OYEN, NIÑOS
LISTEN, CHILDREN

OYEN, NIÑOS
LISTEN, CHILDREN

A unique collection of Mother Goose
rhymes, songs, jingles and riddles
in Spanish and English

By
Grace Barrington Hofer
and
Rachel Pressly Day

Illustrated and designed by
Stephen Moncus

EAKIN PRESS ★ Austin, Texas

FIRST EDITION

Copyright © 1992
By Grace Barrington Hofer
and Rachel Pressly Day

Published in the United States of America
By Eakin Press
An Imprint of Sunbelt Media, Inc.
P.O. Drawer 90159 ★ Austin, TX 78709-0159

ALL RIGHTS RESERVED. No part of this book may be reproduced in any form without written permission from the publisher, except for brief passages included in a review appearing in a newspaper or magazine.

ISBN 0-89015-865-7

10   9   8   7   6   5   4   3   2

Library of Congress Cataloging-in-Publication Data

Mother Goose. English & Spanish. Selections
    Oyen, niños : a unique collection of Mother Goose rhymes, poems, and songs in Spanish and English / [compiled] by Grace Barrington Hofer : translations by Rachel Pressly Day : illustrations by Stephen Moncus.
      p.   cm.
    Summary: A collection of Mother Goose rhymes, poems, songs, and riddles in Spanish and English.
    ISBN 0-89015-865-7 : $12.95
    1. Nursery rhymes — Translations into Spanish. 2. Children's poetry — Translations into Spanish. [1. Nursery rhymes. 2. Spanish language materials — Bilingual.] I. Hofer, Grace Barrington. II. Day, Rachel Pressly. III. Moncus, Stephen, ill. IV. Title.
PZ8.3.M85   1992b
398.8--dc20
                                                    92-19251
                                                         CIP
                                                          AC

For Clair and Clyde,

Shane and Rachel

Acknowledgments

The authors would like to express their gratitude to the following persons who have contributed greatly, in one way or another, in making this book possible: Mary Esther Bernal, director of arts and language, San Antonio Independent School District; Barbara Harper, Spanish instructor, Schreiner College; Margaret Day Koenig, Henry E. Pressly, Jr., John E. Fleckenstein, Sarah Lopez, Irene Gonzales, Rosa Hirons, and Conchita Diez de Castrejon.

Contents — Part I

Twinkle, twinkle, little star, 2
Jack and Jill, 3
Baa, baa, black sheep, 4
Little Miss Muffet, 6
Hey, diddle diddle, 8
The little girl with a curl, 9
Solomon Grundy, 10
A week of birthdays, 11
Thirty days hath September, 12
Cocks crow, 13
Rain, 14
For every evil, 15
Hark, hark, 16
Legs, 17
Dreams, 18
Pat-a-cake, pat-a-cake, 19
Humpty Dumpty, 21
Little pussy, 22
Three little kittens, 24
Five toes, 25
Tom, Tom, the piper's son, 26
Pussy-cat, pussy-cat, 27
Little Jack Horner, 28
Little Boy Blue, 29
Jack, be nimble, 30
A riddle, a riddle, 31
Little Nancy Etticoat, 32
Three wise men of Gotham, 33
Georgy Porgy, 35

Indices — Primera Parte

Brilla, brilla, estrellita, 2
Jack y Jill, 3
Be, be, oveja negra, 4
La chica Miss Muffet, 6
¡Oye, mira!, 8
Una niñita con su rizo, 9
Salomón Grundes, 10
Una semana de cumpleaños, 11
Los meses, 12
Los gallos cantan, 13
La lluvia, 14
Para cada maldad, 15
¡Oye, oye!, 16
Piernas, 17
Sueños, 18
Hazme una gordita, hazme una gordita, 19
Humpty Dumpty, 21
La gatita, 22
Los tres gatitos, 24
Los cinco dedos del pie, 25
Tomás, Tomás, el hijo del gaitero, 26
Gatita, gatita, 27
El pequeño Jack Horner, 28
El pequeño Boy Blue, 29
Juan, debes de ser ligero, 30
Una adivinanza, 31
La chica Nancy Paraguas, 32
Tres sábios de Gotham, 33
Jorji Porji, 35

Contents — Part II

The seven days, 38
The pretty bird, 39
My doll, 41
Songs
   Sweet orange, 42
   The shoemaker, 43
   The chicks, 44
   Little bird, 46
   The spring, 47
   The ant, 49
Button counting, 50
The snake, 51
Ever since I told her, 52
Riddles, 53
A Mexican tale, 64
Jingles for children who want more stories, 66
Statues (a game), 67
Chant for a stubbed toe, 68
Chant for rubbing bumps, 69
An "eeny meeny" rhyme, 71
Mexico's National Anthem, 72
Idioms commonly used in Mexico, 75

Indices — Segunda Parte

Los siete dias, 38
La pájara pinta, 39
Mi muñeca, 40
Canciones
   Naranja dulce, 42
   El zapatero, 43
   Los pollitos, 44
   Pajarillo, 46
   La fuente, 47
   La hormiga, 49
Contando botones, 50
La víbora, 51
Desde que le dejí, 52
Adivinanzas, 53
Un cuento mexicano, 64
Respuestas cuando los niños piden mas cuentos, 66
Encantados (un juego), 67
Canto para un dedo machucado, 68
Canto para porrazos, 69
Rima para escoger, 71
Himno Nacional Mexicano, 72
Modismos dichos en México, 75

PART I

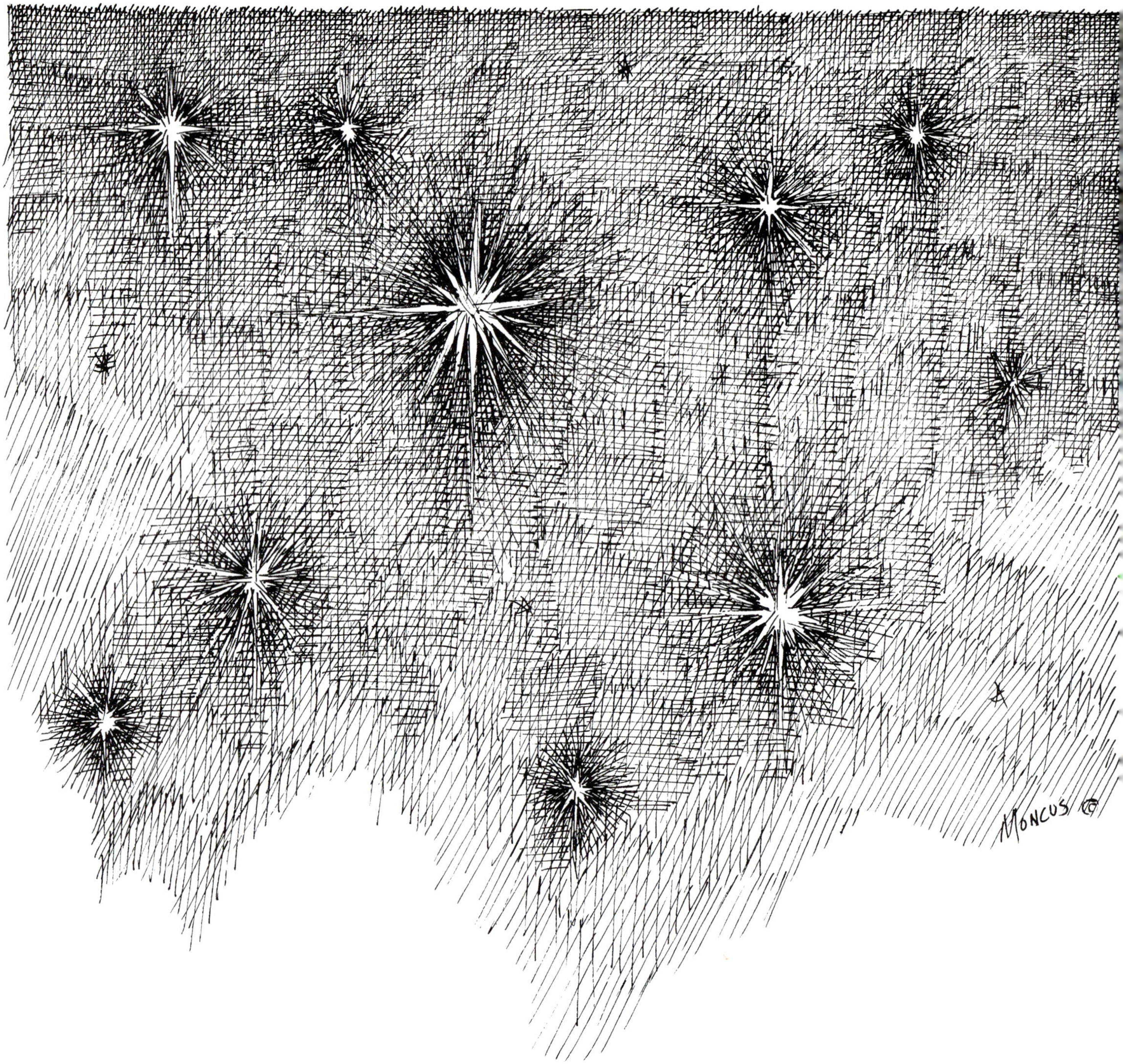

TWINKLE, TWINKLE, LITTLE STAR

    Twinkle, twinkle, little star,
    How I wonder what you are.
    Up above the world so high,
    Like a diamond in the sky.
    Twinkle, twinkle, little star,
    How I wonder what you are.

BRILLA, BRILLA, ESTRELLITA

    Brilla, brilla, estrellita,
    Un milagro, tan bonita.
    Tan lejana, ay te cante,
    En el cielo, un diamante.
    Brilla, brilla, estrellita,
    Un milagro, tan bonita.

JACK AND JILL WENT UP THE HILL

Jack and Jill went up the hill
To fetch a pail of water;
Jack fell down and broke his crown,
And Jill came tumbling after.

JACK Y JILL FUERON AL POZO

Jack y Jill fueron al pozo
Por una cubeta de agua;
Jack se cayó su cráneo rompió,
Y Jill rodeando lo siguió.

BAA, BAA, BLACK SHEEP

Baa, baa, black sheep,
Have you any wool?
Yes sir, yes sir,
Three bags full:
One for my master,
One for my dame,
And one for the little boy
Who lives down the lane.

BE, BE, OVEJA NEGRA

Be, be, oveja negra,
¿Tienes lana tú?
Sí señor, sí señor,
Tres bolsas llenas:
Uno para mi patrón,
Uno para mi dama,
Y uno para el niño
Allá en esa loma.

LITTLE MISS MUFFET

Little Miss Muffet
Sat on a tuffet,
Eating her curds and whey.
There came a big spider
Who sat down beside her
And frightened Miss Muffet away.

LA CHICA MISS MUFFET

La chica Miss Muffet
Buscó un asiento,
Su leche cuajada, a comer.
Pero una araña se acercó
Cerca de ella se sentó
Y la espantó a correr.

HEY, DIDDLE DIDDLE	¡OYE, MIRA!
Hey, diddle diddle,	¡Oye, mira! chapulín,
The cat and the fiddle,	El gato con su violín,
The cow jumped over the moon.	La vaca brincó sobre la luna.
The little dog laughed	El perrito se rió
To see such sport,	Al ver lo que pasó,
And the dish ran away with the spoon.	Y el plato con su cuchara corrió.

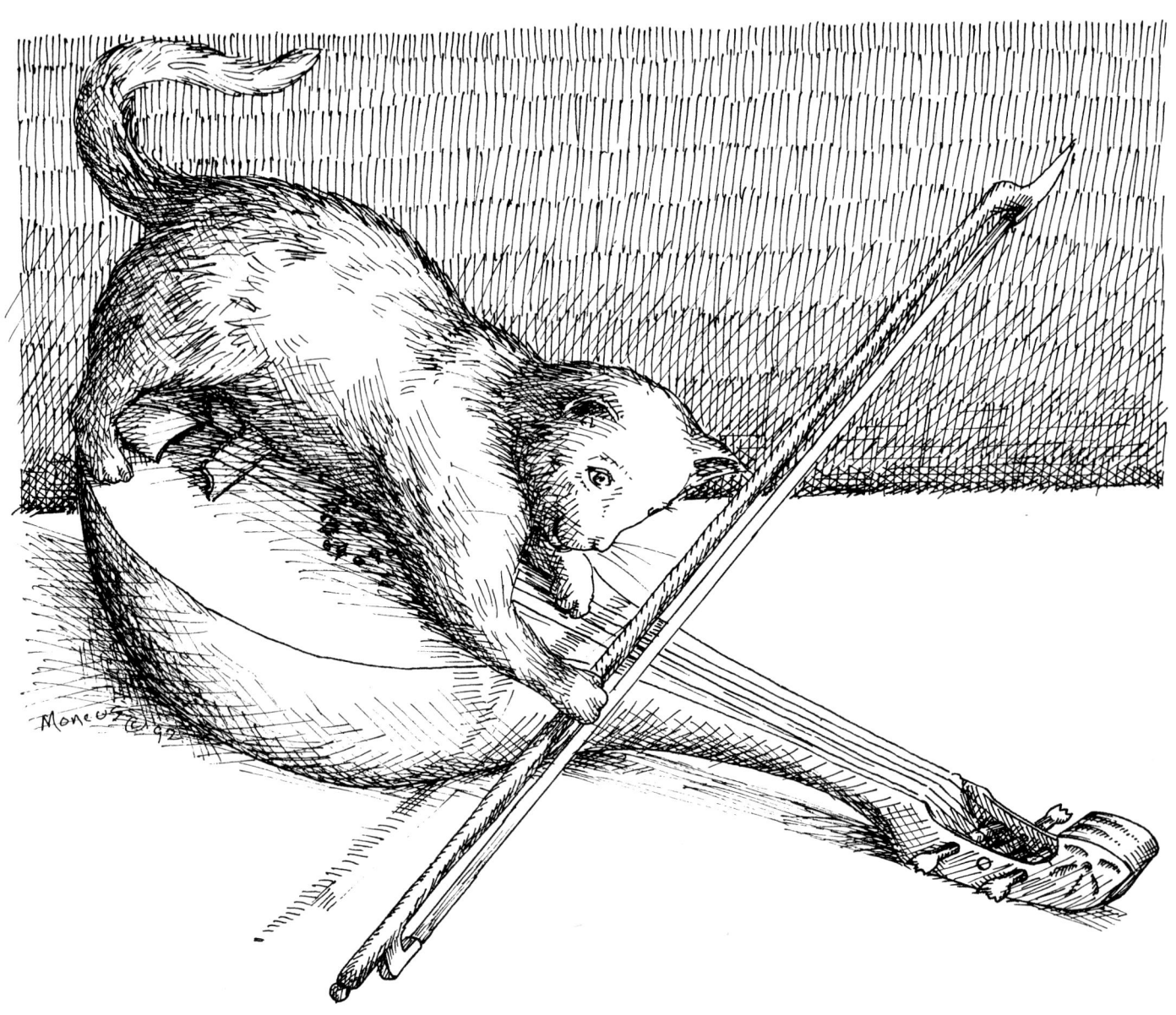

THE LITTLE GIRL
WITH A CURL

There was a little girl
Who had a little curl
Right in the middle of her forehead;
When she was good,
She was very, very good,
And when she was bad
She was horrid.

UNA NIÑITA
CON SU RIZO

*Hay una niñita
Que tiene un rizo
En medio de la frente;
Cuando se comporta bien,
Es muy amable,
Pero cuando se comporta mal
Es muy desagradable.*

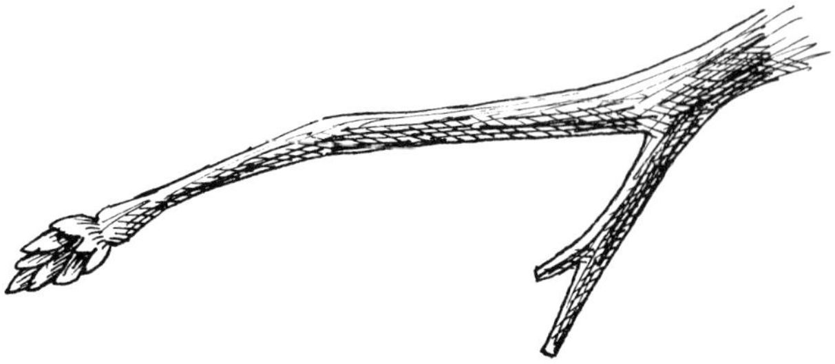

SOLOMON GRUNDY

Solomon Grundy
Born on Monday,
Christened on Tuesday,
Married on Wednesday,
Took ill on Thursday,
Worse on Friday,
Died on Saturday,
Buried on Sunday,
This is the story
Of Solomon Grundy.

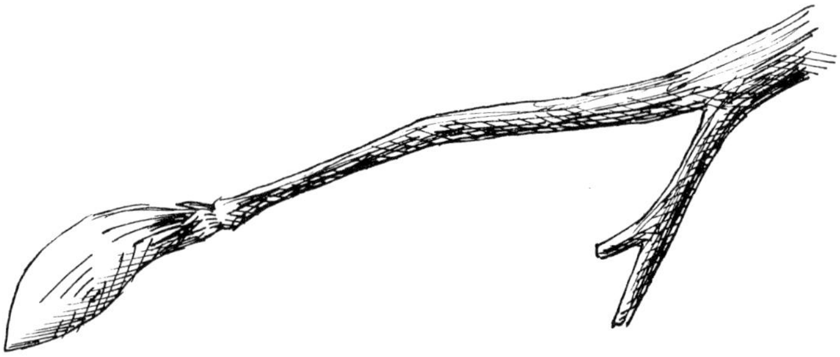

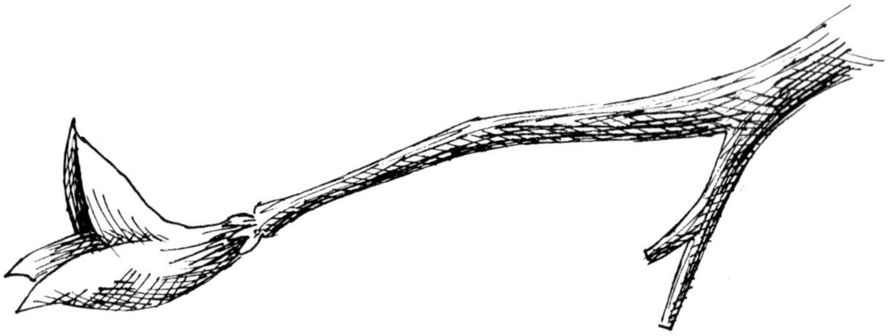

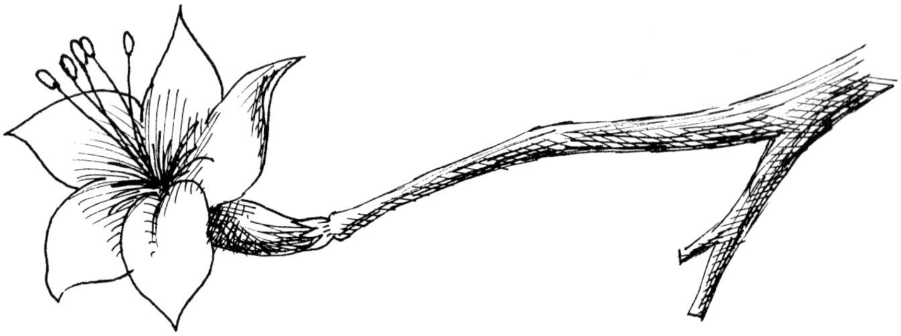

SALOMÓN GRUNDES

Salomón Grundes
Nacido el lunes,
Bautizado el martes,
Cazado el miércoles,
Se enfermó el jueves,
Se empeoró el viernes,
Se murió el sábado,
Fue enterrado el domingo,
Esta es la historia
De Salomón Grundes.

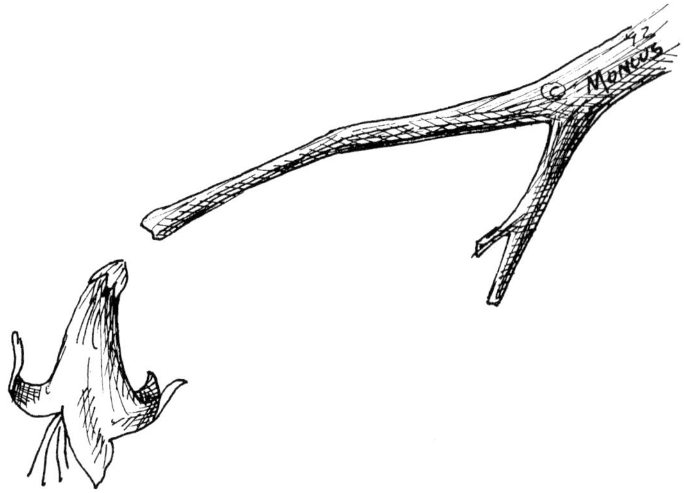

A WEEK OF BIRTHDAYS

Monday's child is fair of face,
Tuesday's child is full of grace,
Wednesday's child is full of woe,
Thursday's child has far to go,
Friday's child is loving and giving,
Saturday's child works hard for its living,
But the child that is born on the Sabbath Day
Is bonny and blithe and good and gay.

UNA SEMANA DE CUMPLEAÑOS

La que nace el lunes es bonita,
La que nace el martes es graciosa,
La que nace el miércoles miseria tendrá,
La que nace el jueves importante saldrá,
La que nace el viernes es amable y bondadosa,
La que nace el sábado en trabajo se engrosa
Pero la que nace el domingo es buena, feliz y hermosa.

THIRTY DAYS HATH SEPTEMBER

Thirty days hath September,
April, June, and November
February has twenty-eight alone;
All the rest have thirty-one,
Excepting leap-year.
That's the time,
When February's days are twenty-nine.

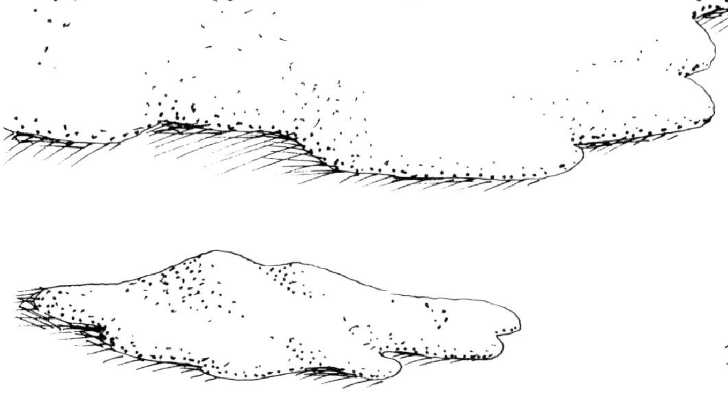

LOS MESES

Treinta días trae septiembre,
Con abril, junio y noviembre
De veintiocho solo hay uno, febrero;
Y los demás de treinta y uno,
Menos el año bisiesto.
Cuando los días de febrero,
Salen ser veintinueve.

COCKS CROW

Cocks crow in the morn
To tell us to rise,
And he who lies late
Will never be wise;
For early to bed
And early to rise,
Is the way to be healthy,
And wealthy and wise.

LOS GALLOS CANTAN

*Los gallos cantan en la madrugada
Para decirnos que nos levantemos,
Y al que se le pega la sábana
Nunca será sabio;
Pero él que se acuesta temprano
Y se levanta temprano,
Tendrá buena salud,
Riquezas y virtud.*

RAIN

Rain, rain, go away,
Come again another day,
Little Johnny wants to play.

LA LLUVIA

*Lluvia, lluvia, vete de aquí,
Regresa otro día en sí,
Porque Juanito quiere jugar así como así.*

FOR EVERY EVIL

For every evil under the sun
There is a remedy or there is none.
If there be one, seek till you find it.
If there be none, never mind it.

PARA CADA MALDAD

Para cada maldad bajo el cielo
O hay remedio o no hay.
Si hay remedio,
Averigua hasta que lo encuentre.
Si no hay, pues buena suerte.

HARK, HARK

Hark, hark, the dogs do bark,
Beggars are coming to town.
Some in jags and some in rags,
And some in velvet gowns.

¡OYE, OYE!

¡Oye, oye! los perros ladran,
Pues los mendigos vienen al pueblo.
Unos en carretas y unos en trapos,
Y unos en trajes de terciopelo.

LEGS	PIERNAS

Two legs for birds
    (showing two fingers)
And you and me.

Four legs for dogs
    (two fingers each hand)
And squirrels in a tree.

Six legs for beetles
    (three fingers each hand)
Away they go.
    (running with fingers)

Eight legs for spiders
    (palms together and eight fingers)
What do you know!

Dos piernas para los pájaros
    (enseñando dos dedos)
Para ti y para mí.

Cuatro piernas para los perros
    (enseñando dos dedos de cada mano)
Y para ardillas en sí.

Seis piernas para escarabajos
    (enseñando tres dedos de cada mano)
Se van así.
    (como corriendo con los dedos)

Ocho piernas para arañas
    (los puños juntos y ocho dedos corriendo)
¡Qué crees de eso!

DREAMS

Friday night's dream
On Saturday told,
Is sure to come true,
Be it never so old.

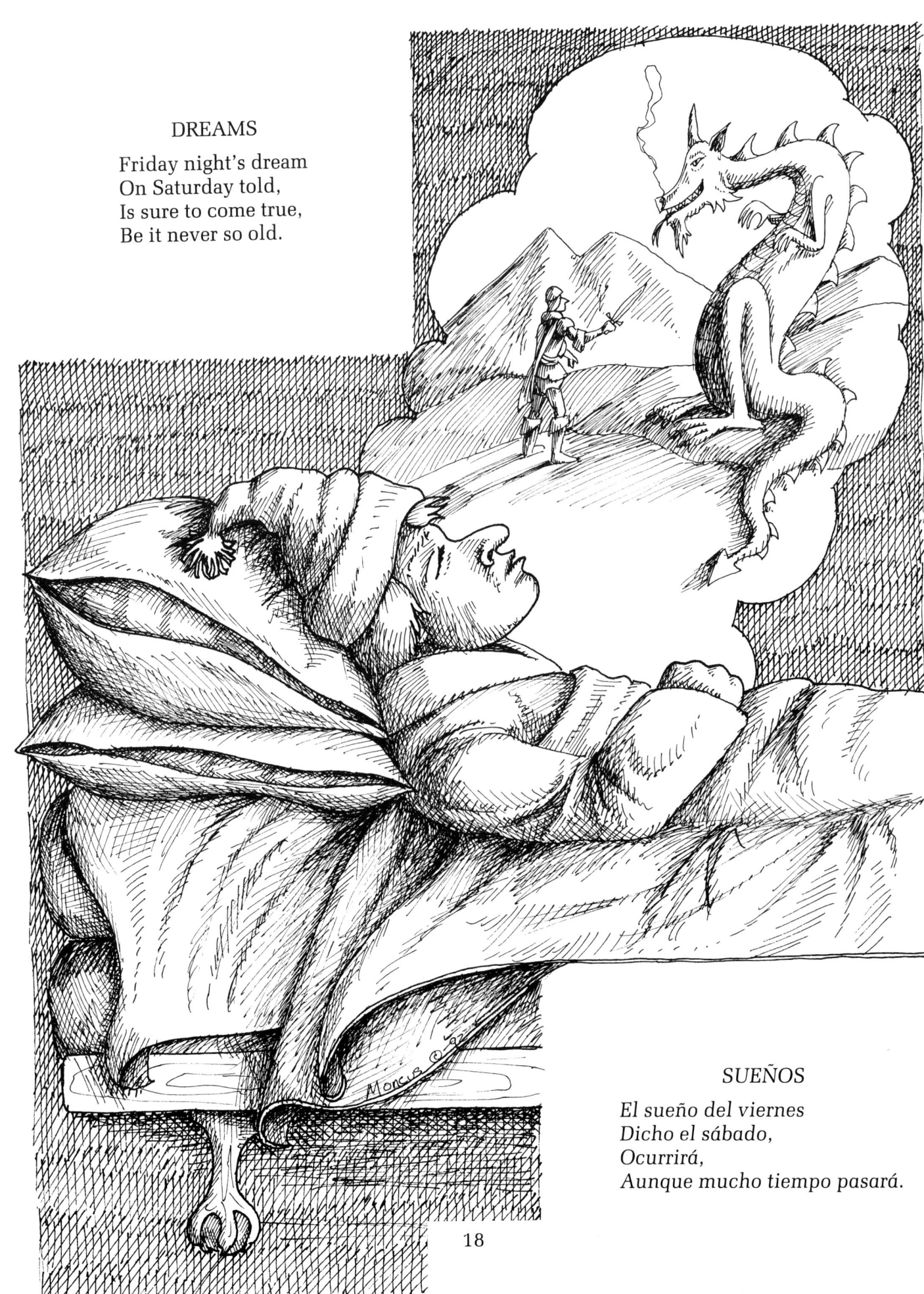

SUEÑOS

El sueño del viernes
Dicho el sábado,
Ocurrirá,
Aunque mucho tiempo pasará.

PAT-A-CAKE, PAT-A-CAKE

Pat-a-cake, pat-a-cake, baker's man,
  (clapping baby's hands together)
Bake me a cake just as fast as you can.
Pat it and prick it and mark it with a B.
  (prick one baby hand, using finger of the other)
Put it in the oven for baby and me.
  (pretend to put both of baby's hands in an oven)

HAZME UNA GORDITA, HAZME UNA GORDITA

Hazme una gordita, hazme una gordita, panadero,
  (palmoteando los manos del bebito)
Hazme un panque tan pronto como puedas.
Palmotéalo, púnzalo y márcalo con una B.
  (marcando una B en una mano)
Y mételo en el horno para mi bebito y para mí.

HUMPTY DUMPTY

Humpty Dumpty sat on a wall,
Humpty Dumpty had a great fall;
All the king's horses and all the king's men
Couldn't put Humpty together again.
    (Since it was an egg)

HUMPTY DUMPTY

Humpty Dumpty en una cerca se sentó,
Pero, por accidente se calló;
Y todos los caballos y todos los hombres del rey
No pudieron recogerlo ni hacerlo completo otra vez.
    (Pues era un huevo)

LITTLE PUSSY

I love little pussy,
Her coat is so warm,
And if I don't hurt her
She'll do me no harm.
I'll sit by the fire
And give her some food,
And pussy will love me
Because I am good.

LA GATITA

Yo quiero a mi gatita,
Tan calientita, su piel,
Y si no le hago daño
Conmigo es bueno él.
Cerca de él me asiento
Para darle de comer,
Y mi acaricio es lento
Pues bueno debo hacer.

THREE LITTLE KITTENS

Three little kittens
Lost their mittens,
And they began to cry,
Oh, mother dear,
We sadly fear
Our mittens we have lost.
What! lost your mittens?
You naughty kittens!
Then you shall have no pie.
Mee-ow, mee-ow, mee-ow.
Three little kittens
They found their mittens
And they began to cry,
Oh, mother dear,
See here, see here,
Our mittens we have found.
What? found your mittens?
You darling kittens,
Then you shall have some pie.

LOS TRES GATITOS

Tres gatitos
Perdieron sus mitones,
Y empezaron a llorar,
Ay, mamá querida,
Tememos que
Hemos perdido nuestros mitones.
¡Qué! ¿perdieron sus mitones?
¡Qué malcreados son!
No les daré pastel.
Miau, miau, miau.
Tres gatitos
Encontraron sus mitones.
Y empezaron a llorar,
Mamacita, querida,
Mira, mira,
Encontramos los mitones.
¿Qué? ¿encontraron sus mitones?
Qué buenos gatitos,
Ahora les daré pastel.

FIVE TOES

This little pig went to market,
　　(yanking big toe)
This little pig stayed home,
　　(yanking second toe, etc.)
This little pig had roast beef,
This little pig had none,
And this little pig cried,
　　(yanking baby toe)
Wee-wee-wee-wee, all the way
　　home.

LOS CINCO DEDOS DEL PIE

Este puerquito fué al mercado,
　　(jalando el dedo grande)
Este puerquito se quedó en la casa,
　　(jalando el segundo dedo, en fin)
Este puerquito tuvo "rosbif,"
A este puerquito no le dieron nada,
Ye este puerquito lloró,
Ui-ui-ui-ui, por una temporada.

TOM, TOM THE PIPER'S SON

Tom, Tom, the piper's son
Stole a pig and away he run.
The pig did bleat and Tom was beat,
And Tom went running down the street.

TOMÁS, TOMÁS, EL HIJO DEL GAITERO

Tomás, Tomás, el hijo del gaitero
Se robó un puerquito y de allí huyó.
El puerquito chilló y Tomás se fue agotado,
Y Tomás corriendo por un lado.

PUSSY-CAT, PUSSY-CAT

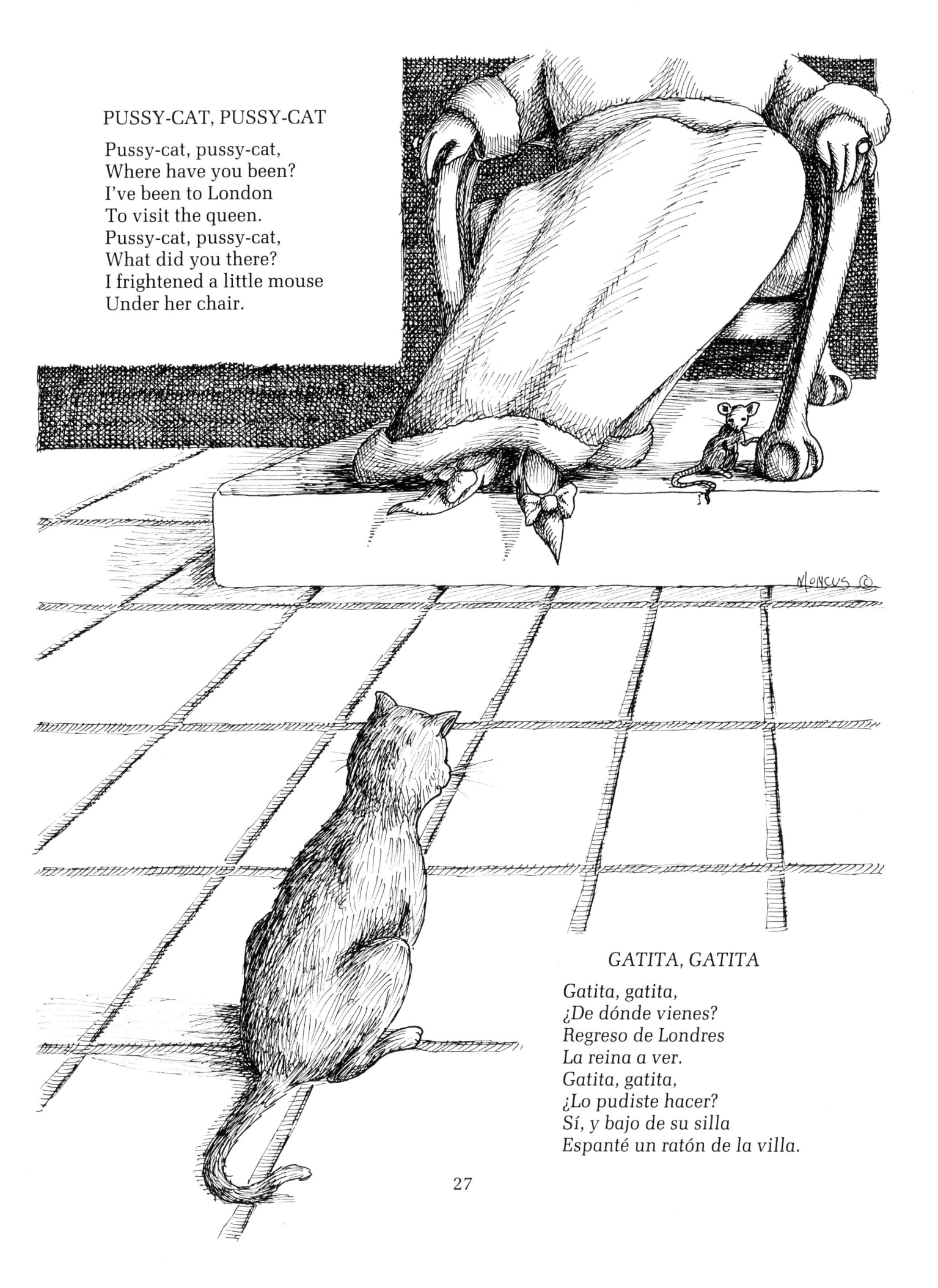

Pussy-cat, pussy-cat,
Where have you been?
I've been to London
To visit the queen.
Pussy-cat, pussy-cat,
What did you there?
I frightened a little mouse
Under her chair.

GATITA, GATITA

Gatita, gatita,
¿De dónde vienes?
Regreso de Londres
La reina a ver.
Gatita, gatita,
¿Lo pudiste hacer?
Sí, y bajo de su silla
Espanté un ratón de la villa.

LITTLE JACK HORNER

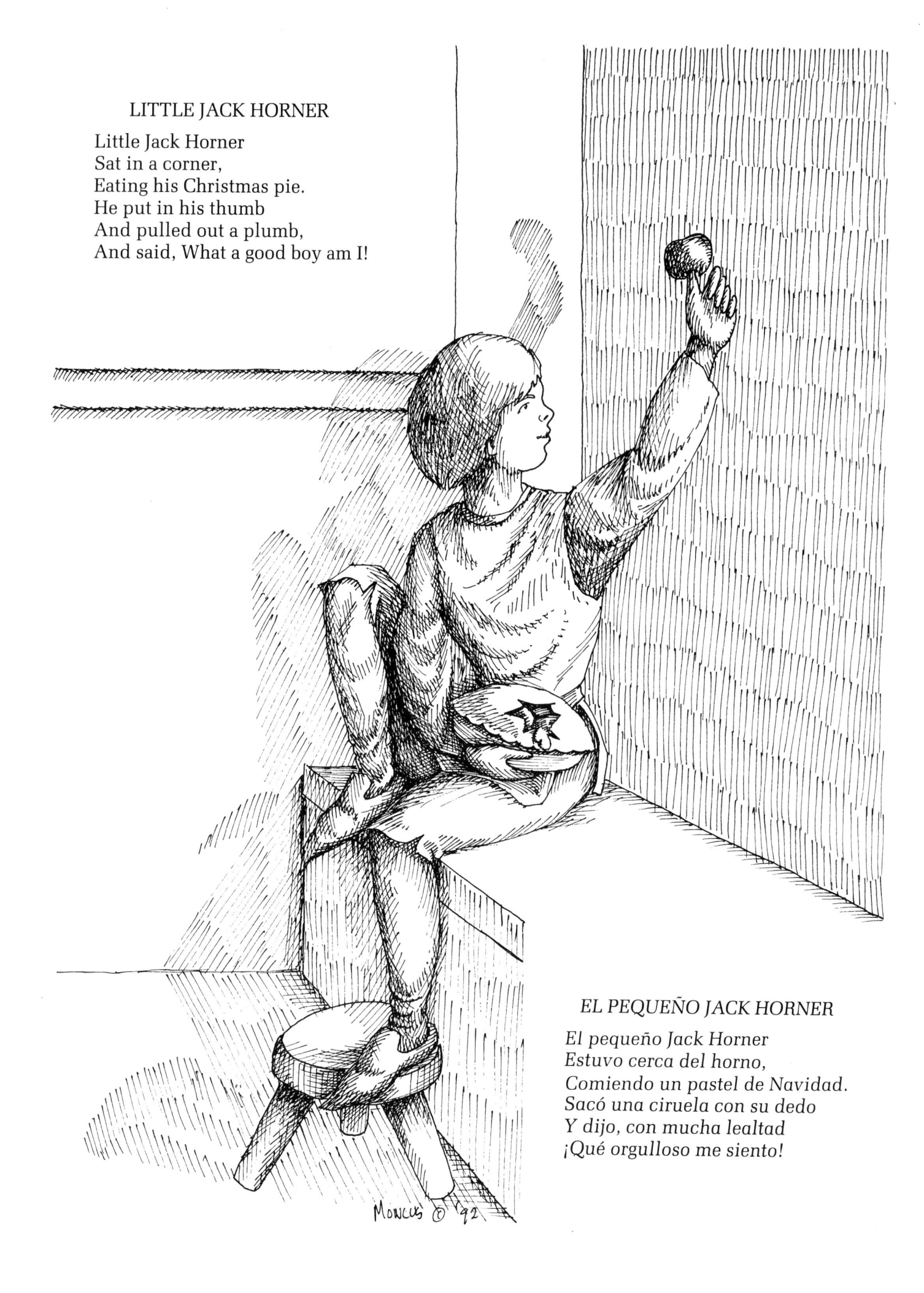

Little Jack Horner
Sat in a corner,
Eating his Christmas pie.
He put in his thumb
And pulled out a plumb,
And said, What a good boy am I!

EL PEQUEÑO JACK HORNER

El pequeño Jack Horner
Estuvo cerca del horno,
Comiendo un pastel de Navidad.
Sacó una ciruela con su dedo
Y dijo, con mucha lealtad
¡Qué orgulloso me siento!

LITTLE BOY BLUE

Little Boy Blue,
Come blow your horn,
The sheep's in the meadow,
The cow's in the corn.
Where is the boy
Who looks after the sheep?
He's under the haystack
Fast asleep.

EL PEQUEÑO BOY BLUE

Oye, pequeño Boy Blue,
Vén y suena tu pito.
Tu oveja está en el prado,
La vaca entre en el maíz.
Donde está el niño
Que guarda los animales?
Estara bajo del almiar
Bien dormido.

JACK, BE NIMBLE

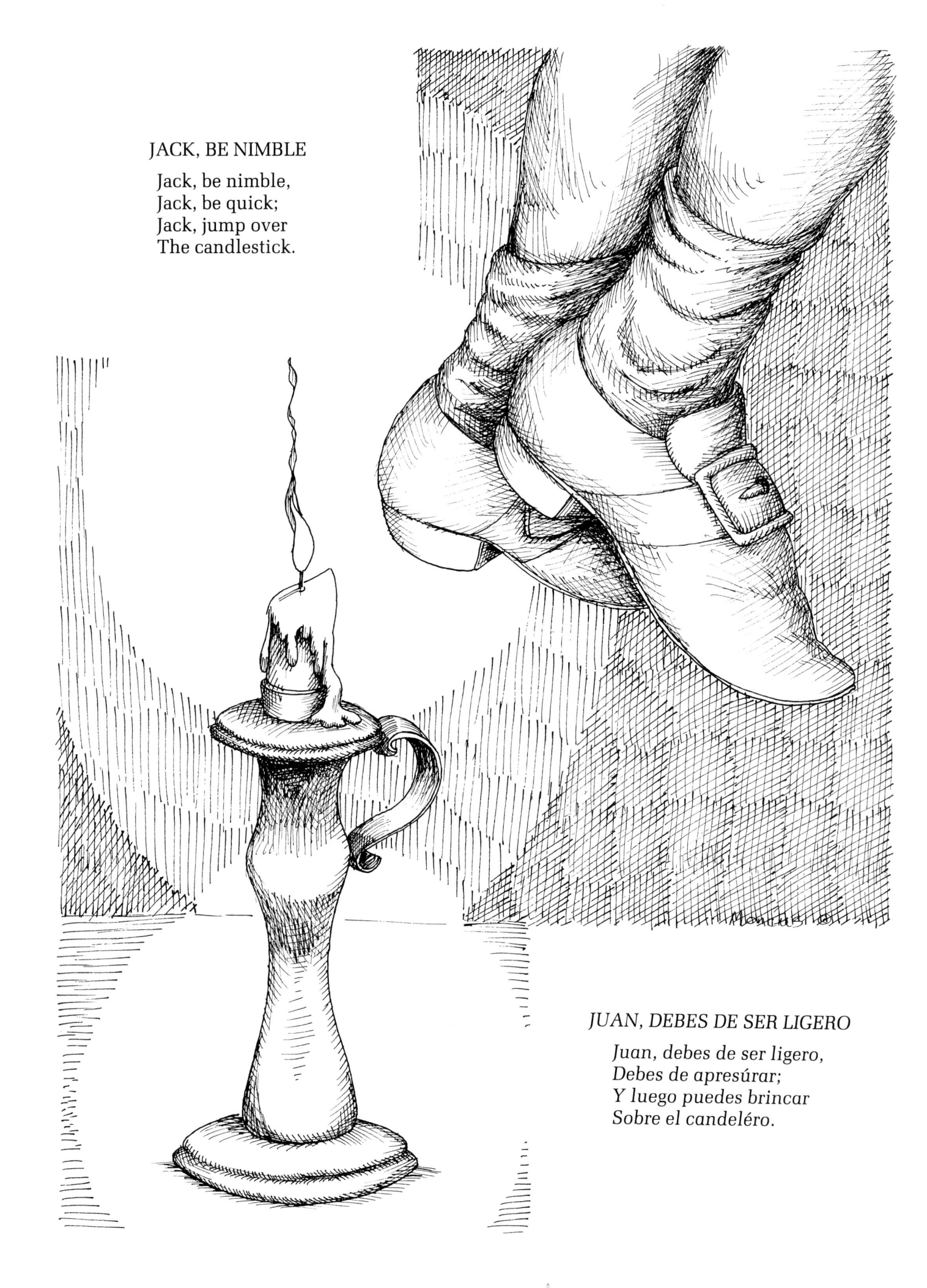

Jack, be nimble,
Jack, be quick;
Jack, jump over
The candlestick.

JUAN, DEBES DE SER LIGERO

Juan, debes de ser ligero,
Debes de apresúrar;
Y luego puedes brincar
Sobre el candeléro.

A RIDDLE, A RIDDLE

A riddle, a riddle
As I suppose,
A hundred eyes
And never a nose.

Answer: A sieve.

UNA ADIVINANZA

*Una adivinanza, una adivinanza
Le propongo,
¿Qué tiene mil de ojos
Y ninguna nariz?*

Respuesta: Un cedazo.

LITTLE NANCY ETTICOAT

Little Nancy Etticoat,
In a white petticoat,
And a red nose.
She has no feet or hands.
The longer she stands
The shorter she grows.

Answer: A candle.

LA CHICA NANCY PARAGUAS

*Chica Nancy Paraguas,
Con sus blancas enaguas,
Y una nariz rosada.
No tiene pies ni manos.
Si se queda parada
Se hace encorvada.*

Respuesta: Una vela.

THREE WISE MEN OF GOTHAM

Three wise men of Gotham
Went to sea in a bowl.
If the bowl had been stronger
My song had been longer.

TRES SABIOS DE GOTHAM

*Tres sabios de Gotham
En una charola se embarcaron.
Pero la charola se rompió
Y mi cuento se acabó.*

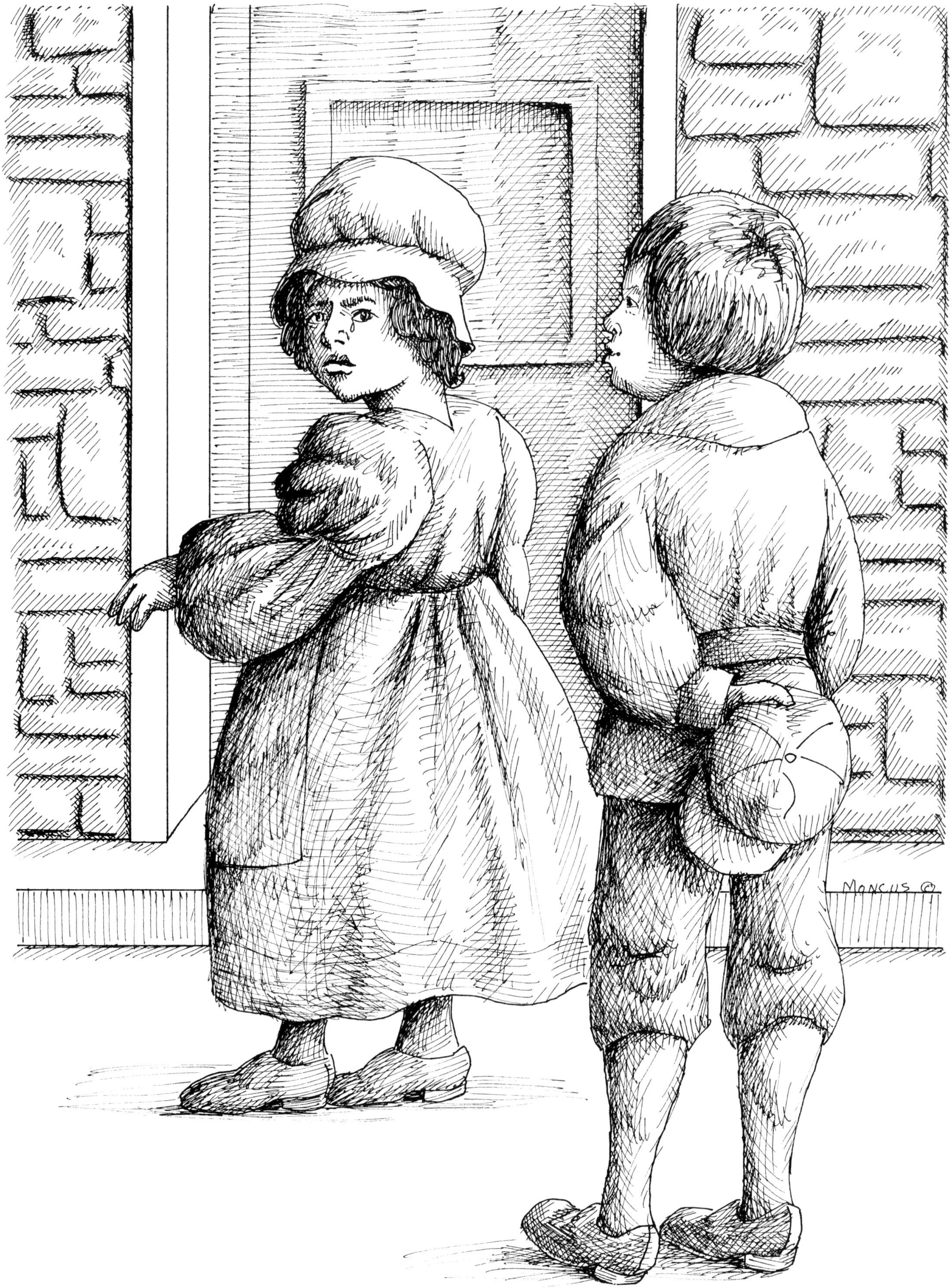
MONCUS ©

GEORGY PORGY

Georgy Porgy, pudding and pie
Kissed the girls and made them cry;
When the boys came out to play,
Georgy Porgy ran away.

JORJI PORJI

*Jorji Porji, pudín y pastel
Besó a las niñas y las hizo llorar;
Pero cuando los niños salieron,
Jorji Porji hulló sin parar.*

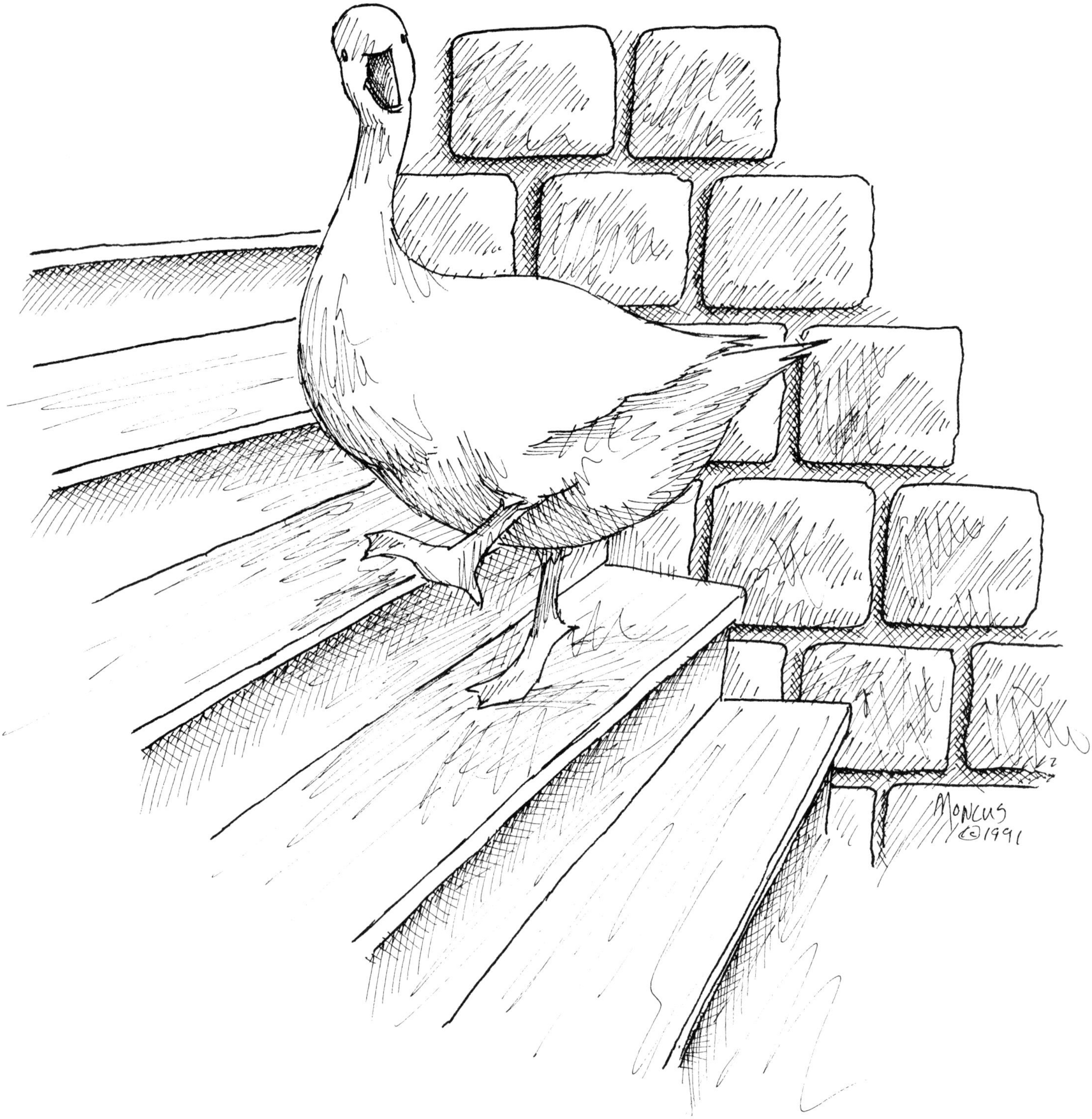
MONCUS
©1991

PART II

SEGUNDA PARTE

LOS SIETE DIAS

Hay en la escuela
Siete niñitos:
Primero, el lunes
Flojo y dormido.
Segundo, el martes
Bueno y activo.
Tercero, el miércoles
Pasa jugando.
Cuarto es jueves
Serio y callado.
Quinto es viernes
Tranquilo y tímido.
Sexto es el sábado
El mas lucido.
Por fin, el domingo
Bello y querido!

THE SEVEN DAYS

There are in school
Seven children:
First, Monday
Lazy and sleepy.
Second, Tuesday
Good and active.
Third, Wednesday
Spends time playing.
Fourth is Thursday
Serious and quiet.
Fifth is Friday
Calm and timid.
Sixth is Saturday
The brightest.
And finally, Sunday
Beautiful and loved!

LA PÁJARA PINTA

Estaba la pájara pinta
Sentada en el verde limón.
Con la cola, meneaba la rama
Y con el pico, picaba la flor.

THE PRETTY BIRD

The pretty colored bird
Was on the green lime tree.
With his tail, he shook the branch
And with his beak, he pecked at the flower.

MI MUÑECA
(una canción para brincar la cuerda)

Tengo una muñeca vestida de azúl
Con sus zapatitos y su manta azúl
La saqué al paséo, se me constipo,
La tengo en su cama con mucho dolor.
Brinca la tablita; yo ya la brinqué.
Bríncala de nuevo; yo ya me cansé.
Dos y dos son cuatro, cuatro y dos son seis,
Seis y dos son ocho y ocho diez-y-seis.

MY DOLL
(sung when jumping rope)

I've got a doll dressed up in blue shoes and cloak.
I took her out for a walk, but she got constipated.
So I have her in bed with much pain.
Jump over the tablet; I've already jumped it.
Jump it again; I'm already tired.
Two and two are four, four and two are six,
Six and two are eight and eight sixteen.

NARANJA DULCE

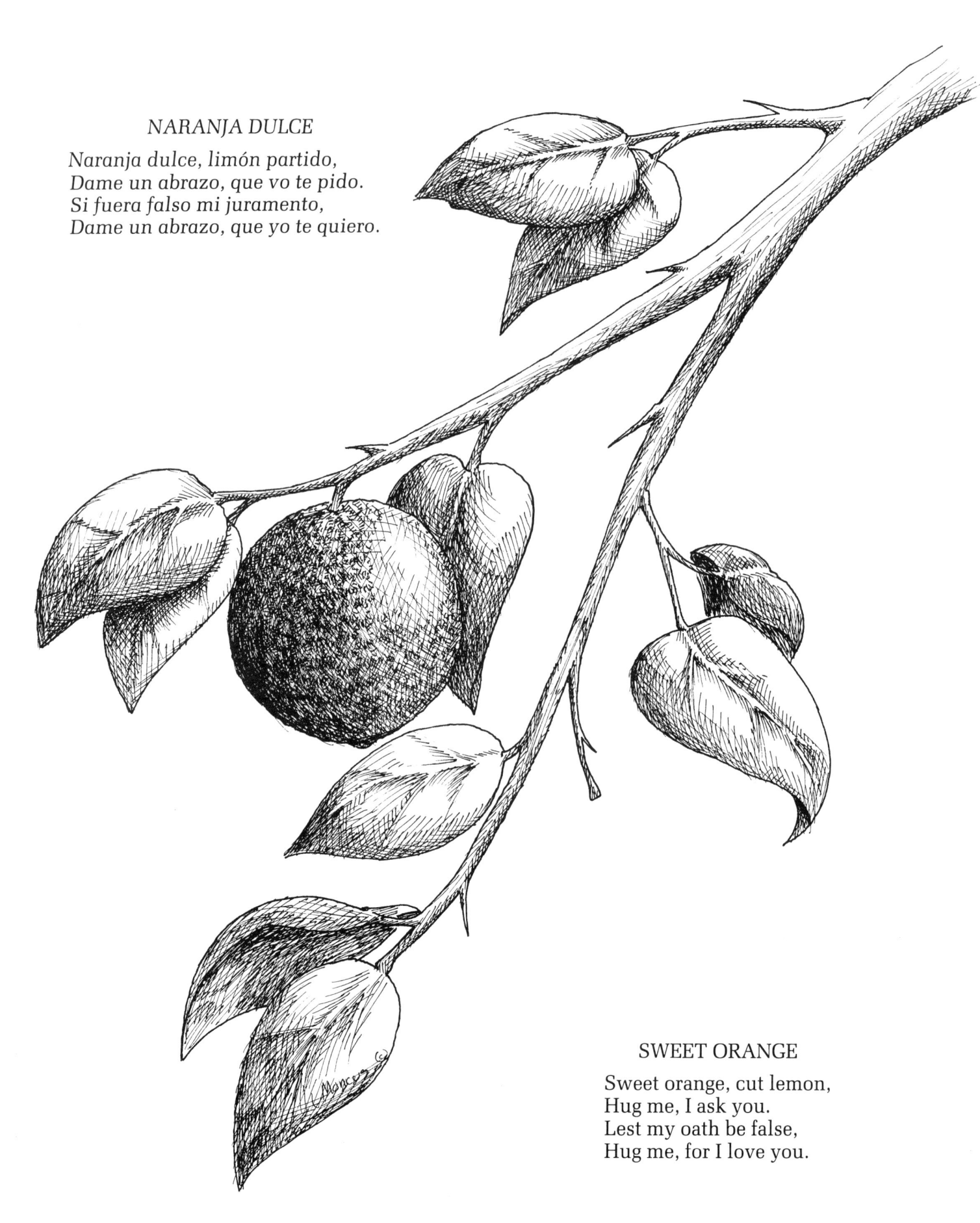

Naranja dulce, limón partido,
Dame un abrazo, que vo te pido.
Si fuera falso mi juramento,
Dame un abrazo, que yo te quiero.

SWEET ORANGE

Sweet orange, cut lemon,
Hug me, I ask you.
Lest my oath be false,
Hug me, for I love you.

EL ZAPATERO

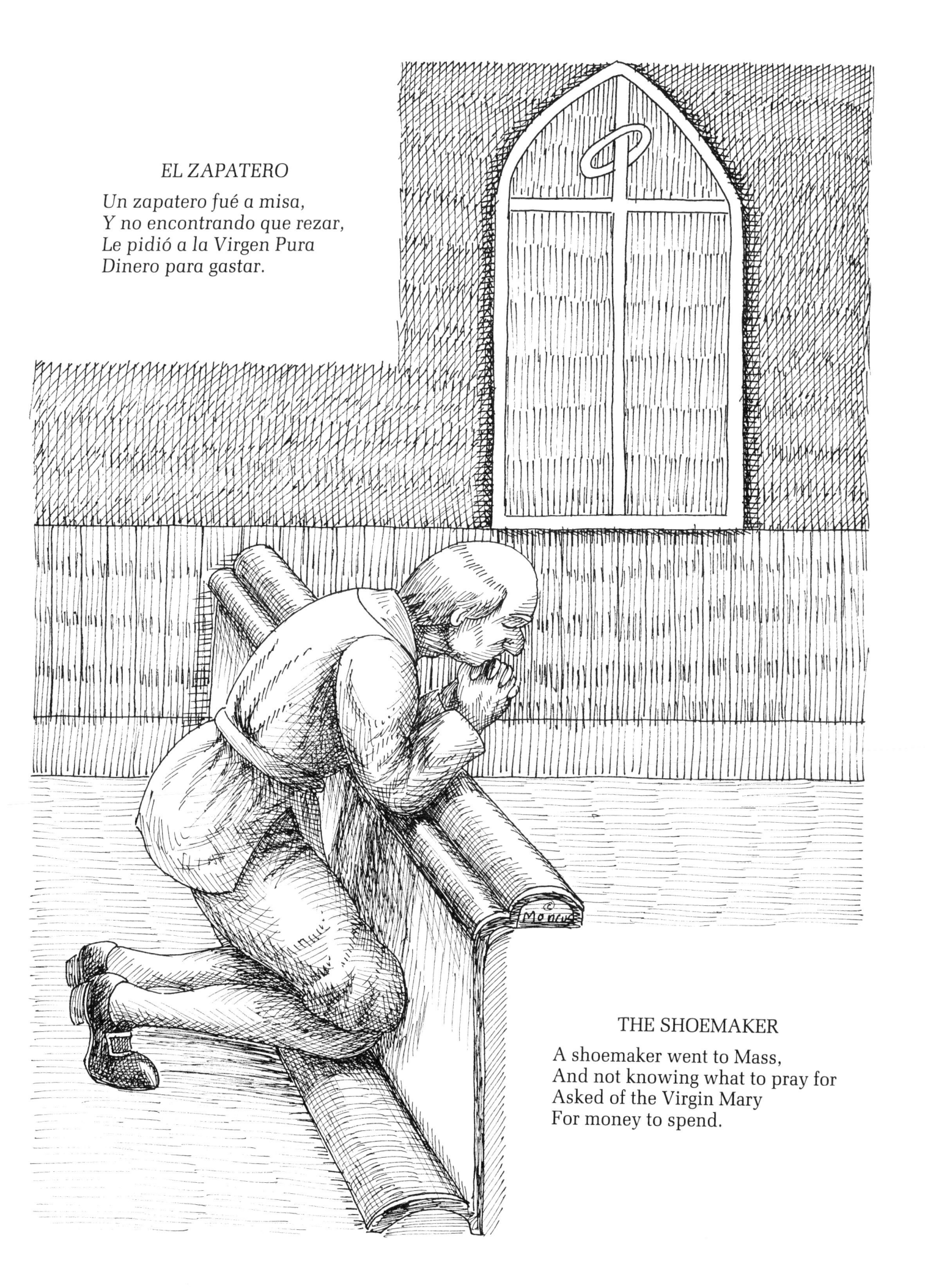

Un zapatero fué a misa,
Y no encontrando que rezar,
Le pidió a la Virgen Pura
Dinero para gastar.

THE SHOEMAKER

A shoemaker went to Mass,
And not knowing what to pray for
Asked of the Virgin Mary
For money to spend.

LOS POLLITOS

Los pollitos dicen,
Pío, pío, pío
Cuando tienen hambre,
Cuando tienen frio.
La gallina busca el maíz y el trigo.
Les da su comida y les presta abrigo.
Bajo de sus alas acurrucaditos,
Duermen les pollitos hasta el otro día.

THE CHICKS

The little chicks say,
Peep, peep, peep
When they are hungry,
When they are cold.
The hen looks for the corn and the wheat.
She feeds them and lends them cover under
 her wings.
They snuggle and sleep until the next day.

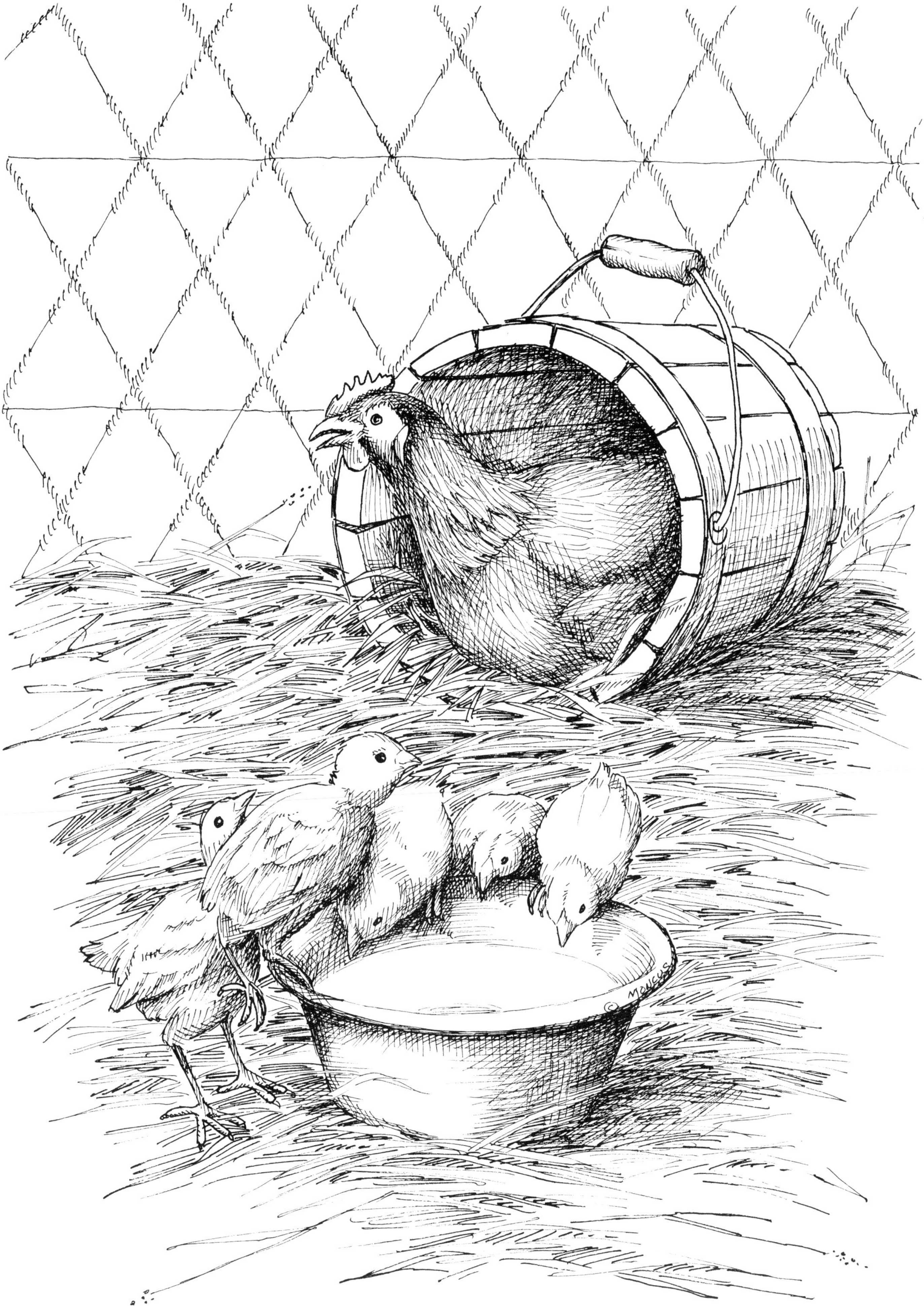

PAJARILLO

Pajarillo, pajarillo,
Que cantá en aquella líma,
Anda díle que no cante
Que el corazon me lastíma.

LITTLE BIRD

Little bird, little bird,
That's singing in the lime tree,
Go tell it to stop singing
For my heart is breaking.

LA FUENTE

Allá en la fuente
Había un chorrito,
Se hacía grandote
Se hacía chiquito.
Estaba de mal humor,
Pobre chorrito,
Tenía calor.

THE SPRING

Over in the spring
There was a current,
Which would at a time be wide
And at a time be thin.
It became bad tempered,
Poor little current,
Because it was hot.

48

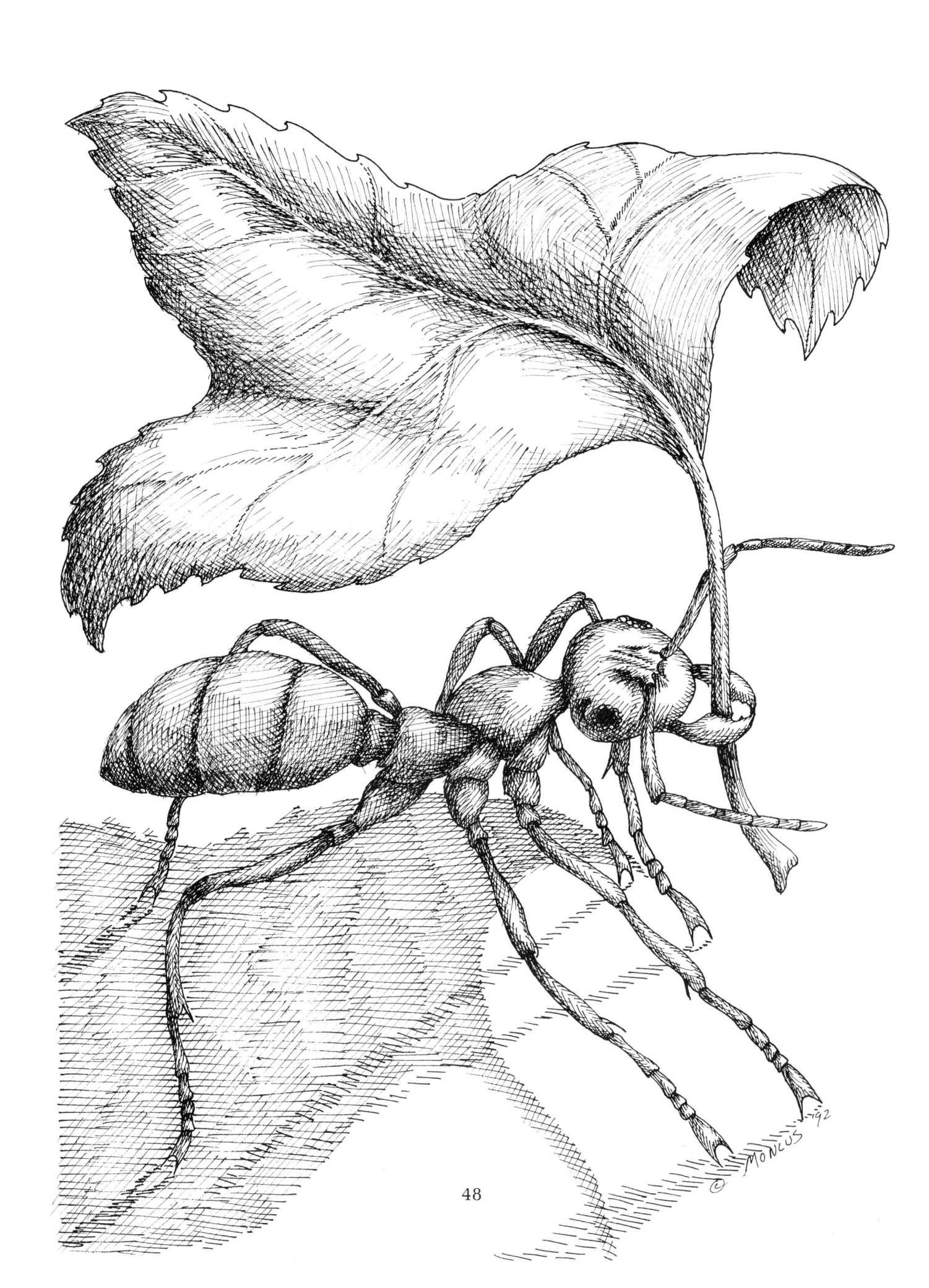

LA HORMIGA

Ay va la hormiga,
Con su paraguas,
Y recogiéndose
Las enaguas.
Estaba de mal humor,
Pobre hormiga,
Tenía calor.

THE ANT

There goes an ant,
With her umbrella,
Holding up
Her petticoats.
She was bad tempered,
Poor little ant,
Because she was hot.

CONTANDO BOTONES

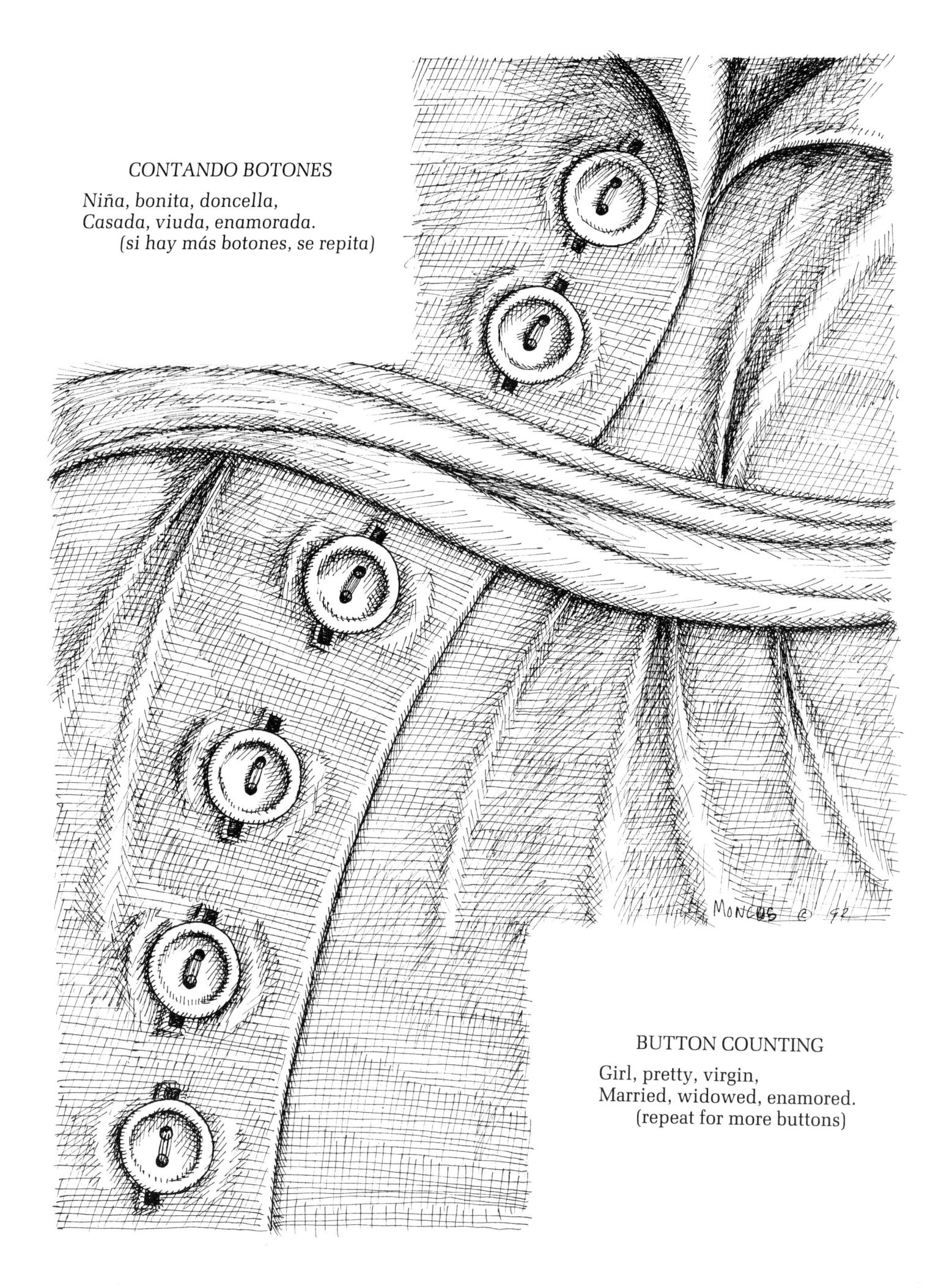

Niña, bonita, doncella,
Casada, viuda, enamorada.
(si hay más botones, se repita)

BUTTON COUNTING

Girl, pretty, virgin,
Married, widowed, enamored.
(repeat for more buttons)

LA VÍBORA

A la víbora, víbora de la mar
Por aquí pueden pasar.
Los de adelante corren mucho
Los de atrás se quedarán.
Tras, tras, tras, tras
    (hasta que agarren un niño)

THE SNAKE

The snake, the snake of the sea
May pass through here.
The first part runs fast
The back end will follow.
Tramp, tramp, tramp, tramp
    (until a child is caught — a
    London Bridge type of game)

DESDE QUE LE DEJI
Dicen que un pobre indio sin educación dijo lo que sigüe:

Desde que le dejí
Que se casara con yo,
Fue cuando supí
Que estaba enamorada de mí.
Mas su genio fue ansí
Que todo lo descompusio,
Y el amor que le tuví
Todavía la estoy tuviendo.

EVER SINCE I TOLD HER
A poor, uneducated man is supposed to have recited the following poem:

Ever since I told her
That she should marry me,
That's when I knew
That she was in love with me.
But her temper was such
That she ruined everything,
And the love I had for her I still have.

PART III

ADIVINANZAS

RIDDLES

Agua pasa por mi casa
Cate de mi corazón.
Respuesta: Aguacate.

"Agua" passes by my house
"Cate" of my heart.
Answer: Aguacate (Avocado).

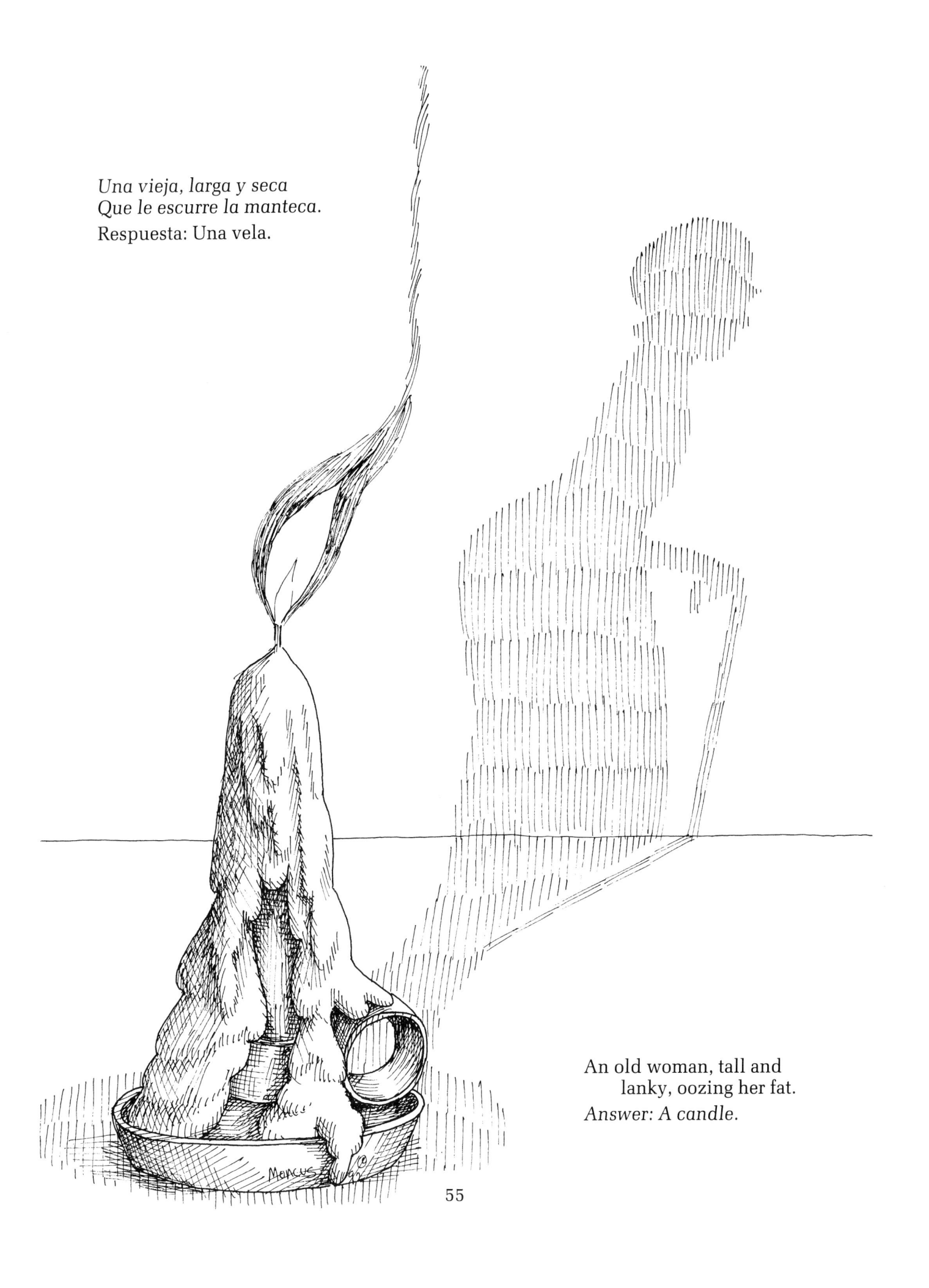

Una vieja, larga y seca
Que le escurre la manteca.
Respuesta: Una vela.

An old woman, tall and
lanky, oozing her fat.
Answer: A candle.

Una señora, muy aseñorada
Con muchos remiendos
Y ninguna puntada.
Respuesta: *Una gallina.*

A woman, very "well to do"
With much pomposity
But little reason for it.
Answer: A hen.

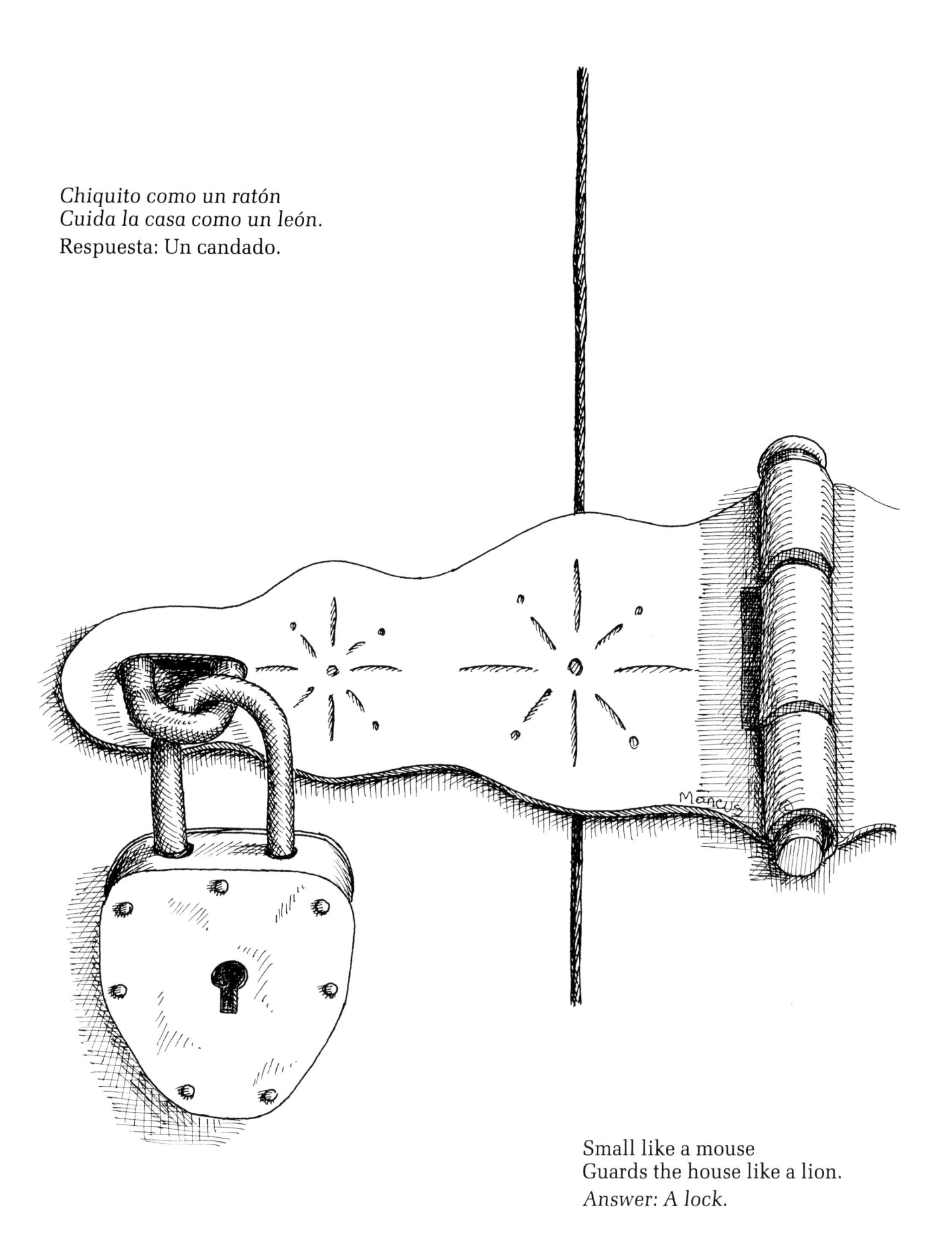

Chiquito como un ratón
Cuida la casa como un león.
Respuesta: Un candado.

Small like a mouse
Guards the house like a lion.
Answer: A lock.

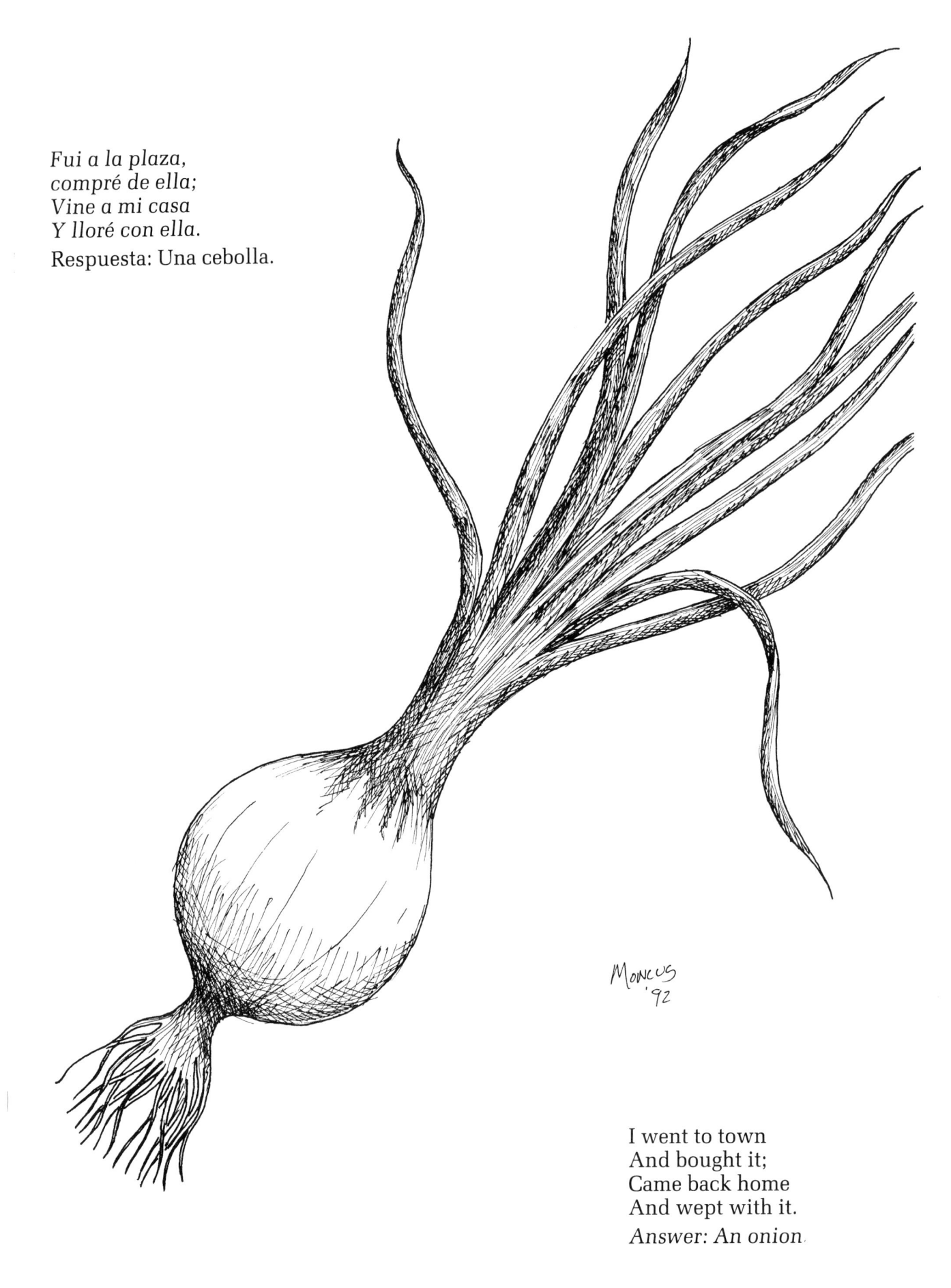

*Fui a la plaza,
compré de ella;
Vine a mi casa
Y lloré con ella.*
Respuesta: Una cebolla.

I went to town
And bought it;
Came back home
And wept with it.
Answer: An onion.

*Largo, largo
Y muy amartillado.*
Respuesta: El camino.

Long as never
Pounded ever.
Answer: The road.

Siempre quietas,
Siempre inquietas,
Durmiendo de día,
De noche despiertan.
Respuesta: Las estrellas.

Always quiet,
Always disquieting,
In daytime sleeping,
At night awakening.
Answer: The stars.

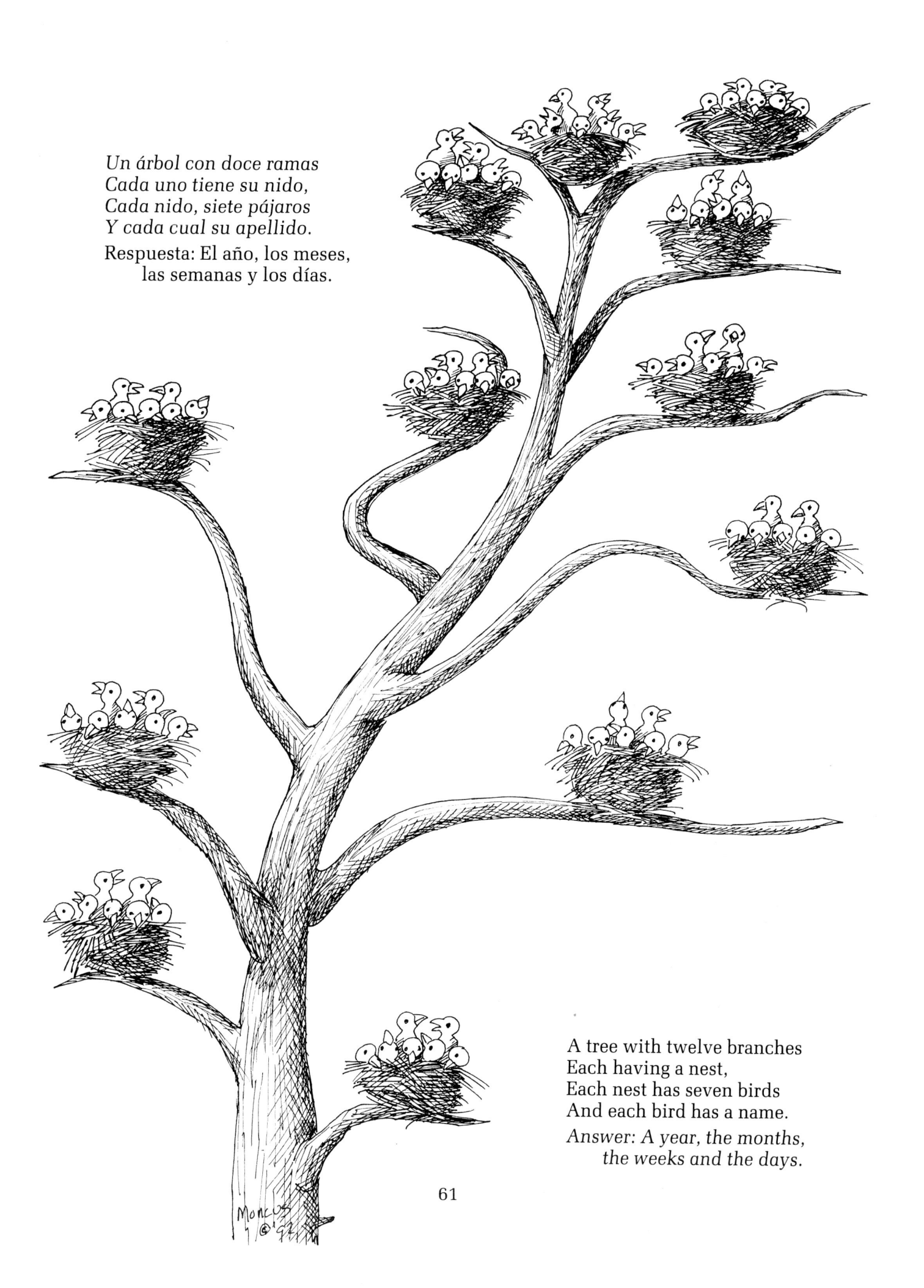

*Un árbol con doce ramas
Cada uno tiene su nido,
Cada nido, siete pájaros
Y cada cual su apellido.*

Respuesta: El año, los meses,
    las semanas y los días.

A tree with twelve branches
Each having a nest,
Each nest has seven birds
And each bird has a name.

*Answer: A year, the months,
    the weeks and the days.*

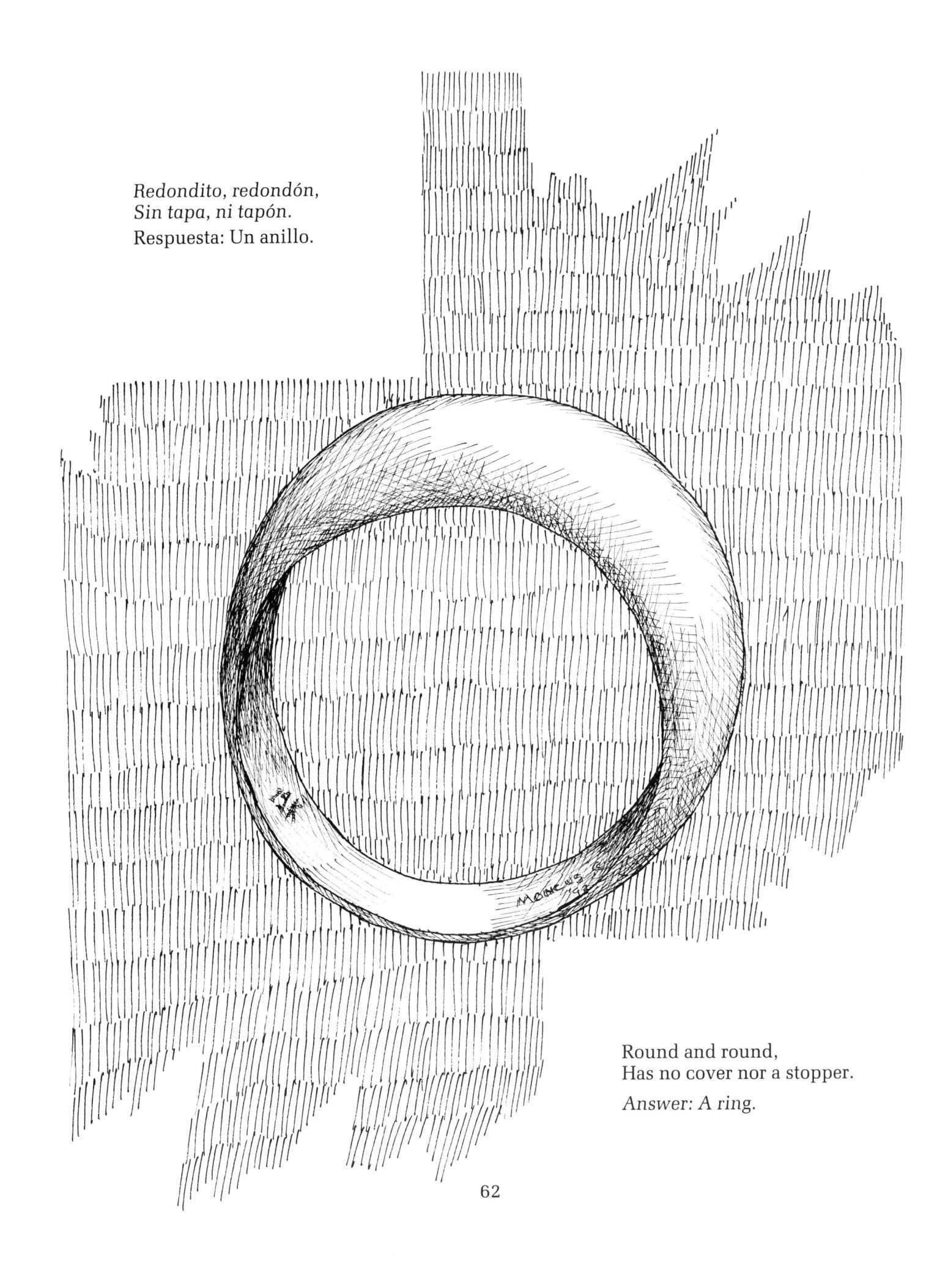

Redondito, redondón,
Sin tapa, ni tapón.
Respuesta: Un anillo.

Round and round,
Has no cover nor a stopper.

Answer: A ring.

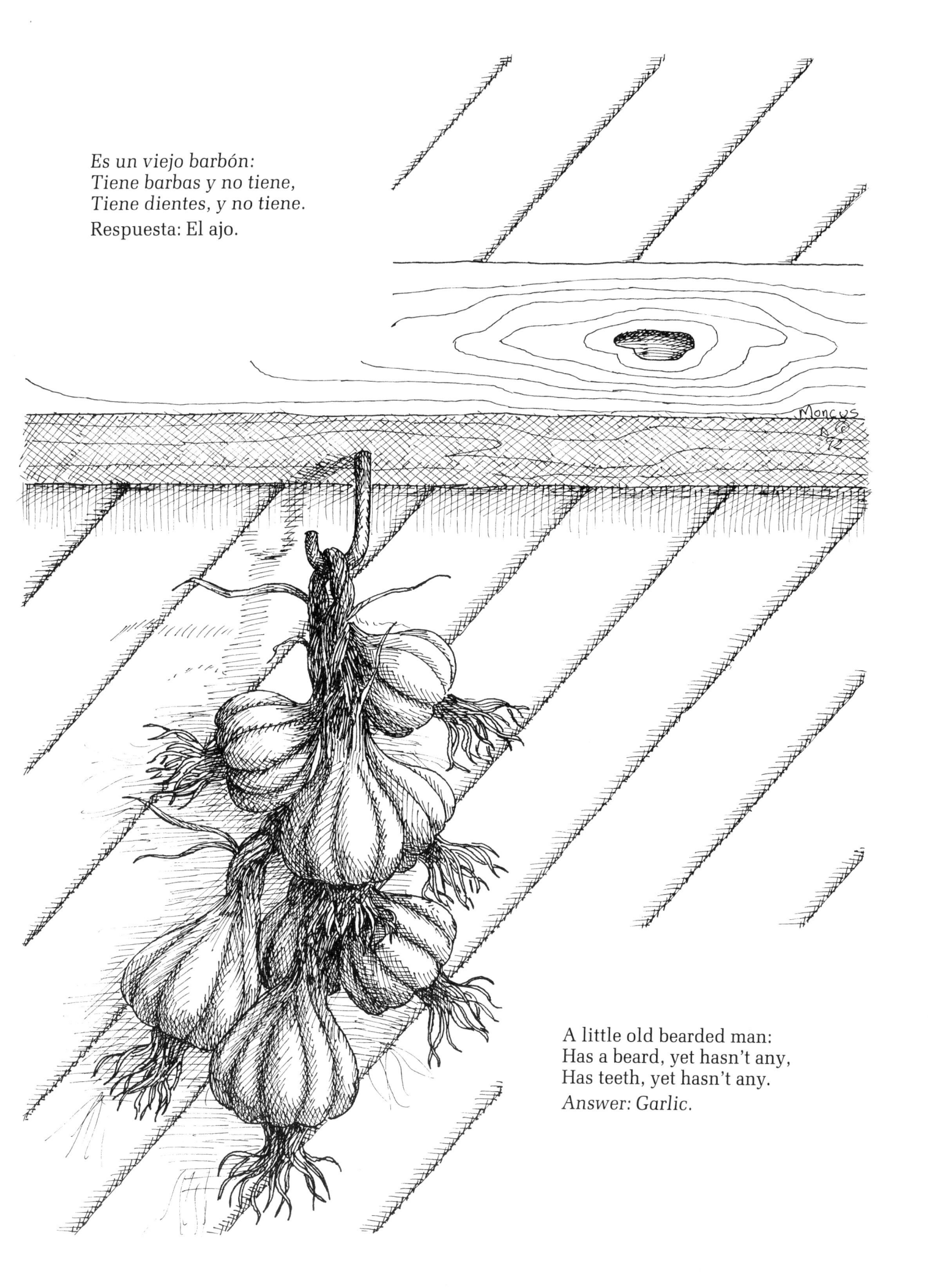

Es un viejo barbón:
Tiene barbas y no tiene,
Tiene dientes, y no tiene.
Respuesta: El ajo.

A little old bearded man:
Has a beard, yet hasn't any,
Has teeth, yet hasn't any.
Answer: Garlic.

UN CUENTO MEXICANO

Si vas al viejo bosque, en su interior,
Verás muchos perritos con su professor,
Don Pipirulando.
Los está enseñando. Ellos todos quieren
aprender.
Si pongo una M, luego una A y luego lo
repito, dirá MAMÁ.
Sonrieron los perritos por la facilidad,
Y todos muy contentos dijeron, Wow,
wow, wow.

A MEXICAN TALE

If you go to the old woods, deep inside,
You will see many puppies with their
professor, Mr. Pipirulando.
He is teaching them. They all want to learn.
If I put an M, then an A and repeat it, it will
say MAMA.
They laugh because of its simplicity,
And all very happily say, Bow, wow, wow.

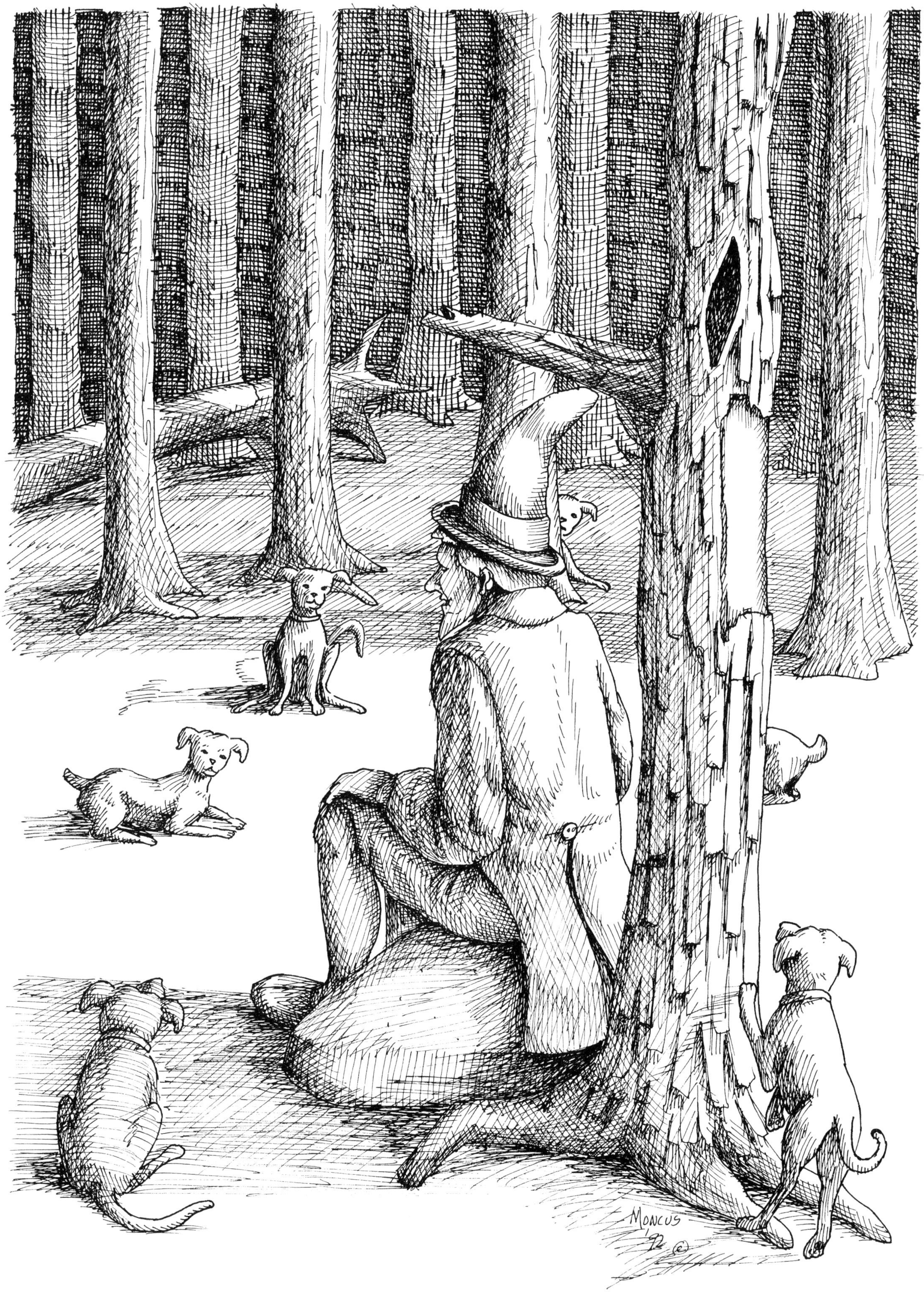
MONCUS
'92 ©

RESPUESTAS CUANDO LOS NIÑOS PIDEN MAS CUENTOS

Había un gato
Con los pies de trapo
Y los ojos al reves;
¿Quieres que te lo cuente otra vez?

Colorín, colorado
El cuento está acabado.

JINGLES FOR CHILDREN WHO WANT MORE STORIES

There was a cat
With ragged paws
And crossed eyes;
Do you want me to tell it again?

Worry, lory, gory,
This is the end of my story.

ENCANTADOS
(un juego)

Pipiripin de San Agustín,
El rey pasó por aquí
Y me dijo que te pusieras así.

    (El que dirige repita esta rima con cada niños y los ponen en una postura ridicula. El que se queda bien sin reir sigue dirigiendo.)

STATUES
(a game)

Peeperepeen of St. Augustine,
The king came by here and said
That you must stand this way.

    (The leader twirls each child into a ridiculous position. He who maintains his stance without laughing is chosen to be the next leader.)

*CANTO PARA
UN DEDO MACHUCADO*

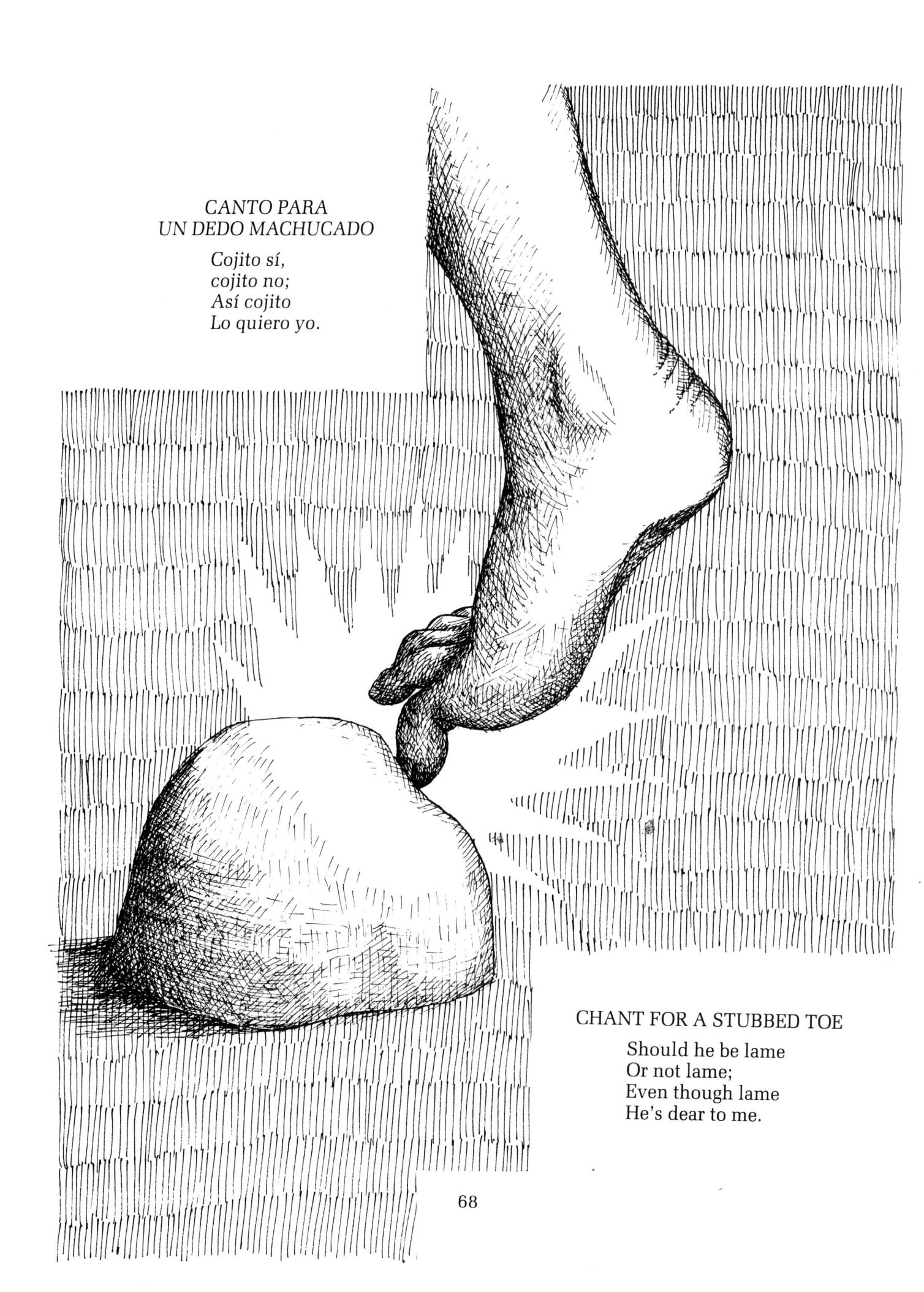

*Cojito sí,
cojito no;
Así cojito
Lo quiero yo.*

CHANT FOR A STUBBED TOE

Should he be lame
Or not lame;
Even though lame
He's dear to me.

CANTO PARA PORRAZOS
(frote al derredor)

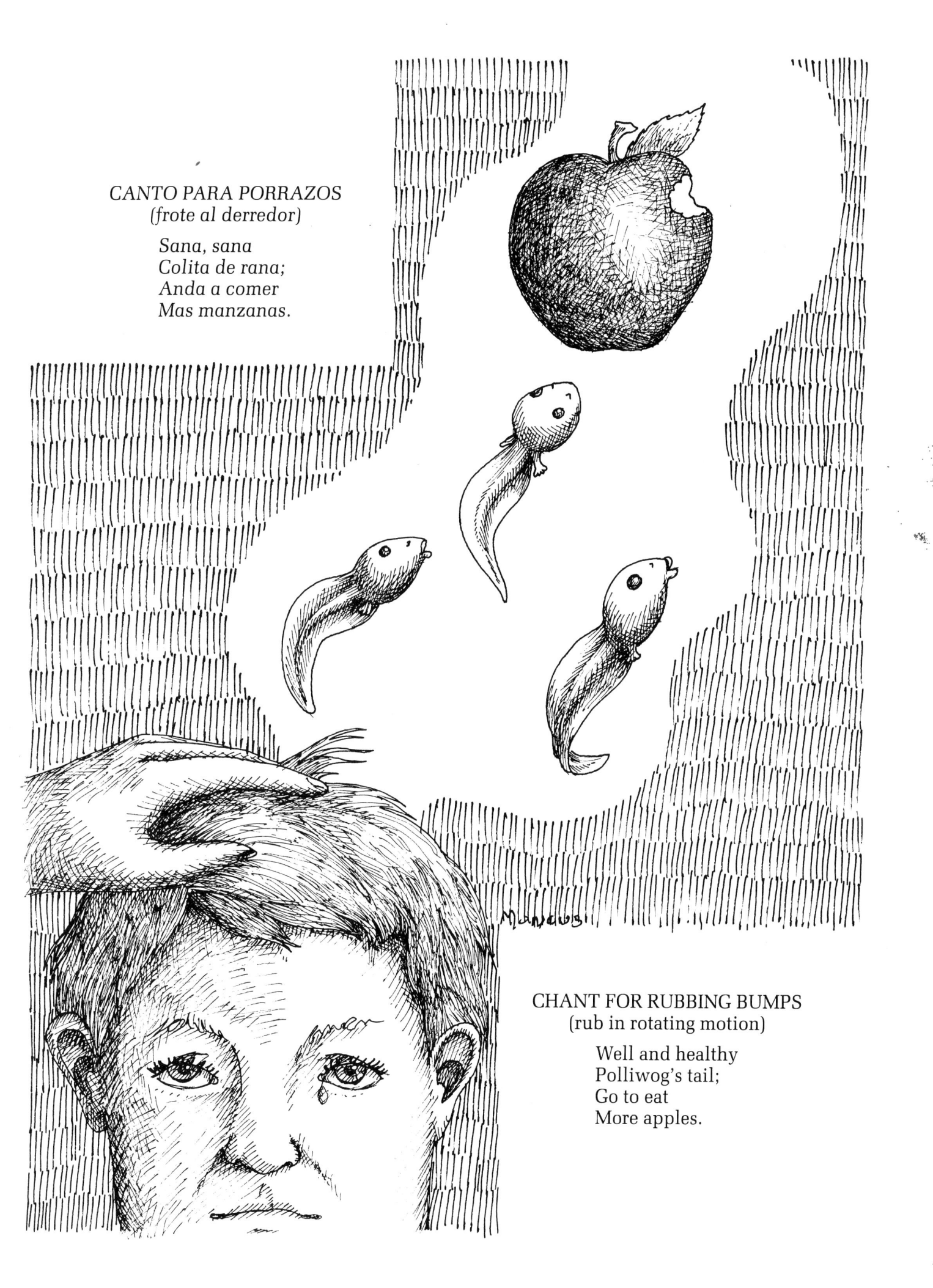

> Sana, sana
> Colita de rana;
> Anda a comer
> Mas manzanas.

CHANT FOR RUBBING BUMPS
(rub in rotating motion)

> Well and healthy
> Polliwog's tail;
> Go to eat
> More apples.

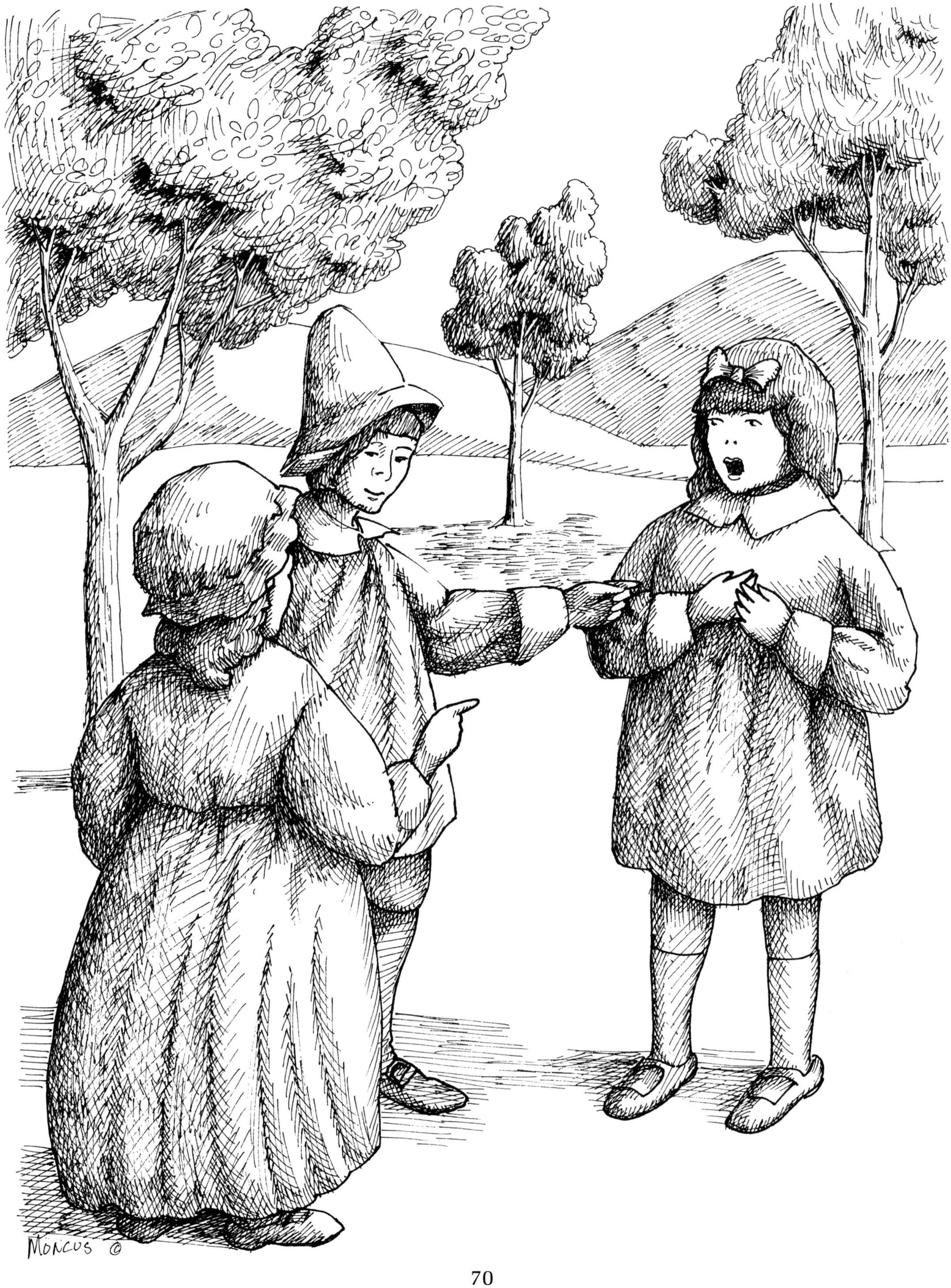
Moncus ©

RIMA PARA ESCOGER

Tin, marín de Don Pingüé;
Cúcara, mácara, pipiri fue.
Yo no fui, fue Teté.
¡Pégale, pégale, que ella fue!

AN "EENY-MEENY" RHYME

Teen, mareen of Don Pingue;
Coocara, macara, peeperee, yea!
I didn't do it, it was Teté.
Spank her, spank her, she did it!

HIMNO NACIONAL MEXICANO
Francisco Gonzales Bocanegra
1824–1861

Coro

Mexicanos al grito de guerra
El acero aprestad y el brindon,
Y retiemble en sus centros la tierra
Al sonoro rugir del cañón.

Verso

¡Cina, oh patria! Tus sienes de oliva
De la paz el arcángel divino,
Que en el cielo tu eterno destino
Por el dedo de Dios se escribió.

Coro: Mexicanos, etc.

Verso

Mas si osare un extraño enemigo
Profanar con su planta tu suelo,
¡Piensa, oh patria querida! quel cielo
Un soldado en cada hijo te dió.

Coro: Mexicanos, etc.

Verso

¡Patria, patria! Tus hijos te juran
exhalar en tus aras aliento,
si el clarín con su bélico acento
los convoca a lidiar con valor.

¡Para tí los guirnaldas de oliva!
¡Un recuerdo para ellos de gloria!
¡Un laurel para tí de victoria!
¡Un sepulcro para ellos de honor!

Coro: Mexicanos, etc.

MEXICO'S NATIONAL ANTHEM
Translation by Rachel Day

Chorus

Mexicans, at the call of war,
Prepare and offer your sword,
For the earth's deep foundations will tremble at the loud rumble of the cannon.

Verse

Oh, homeland! Your brow wears the olive branches
Of the peace the Divine Archangel,
For in the heavens your destiny
Was written by God's own hand.

Chorus: Mexicans, etc.

Verse

But should I venture to banish the enemy that defiles with his foot your land,
Know, oh dear country, that the heavens gave you a soldier in each (of your) sons.

Chorus: Mexicans, etc.

Verse

Homeland! Your children have vowed to breathe in themselves courage should the clarion with its warlike sounds call them together to fight bravely.

For you the wreaths of olive!
A remembrance for them of glory!
For you a victorious laurel!
A grave of honor for them!

Chorus: Mexicans, etc.

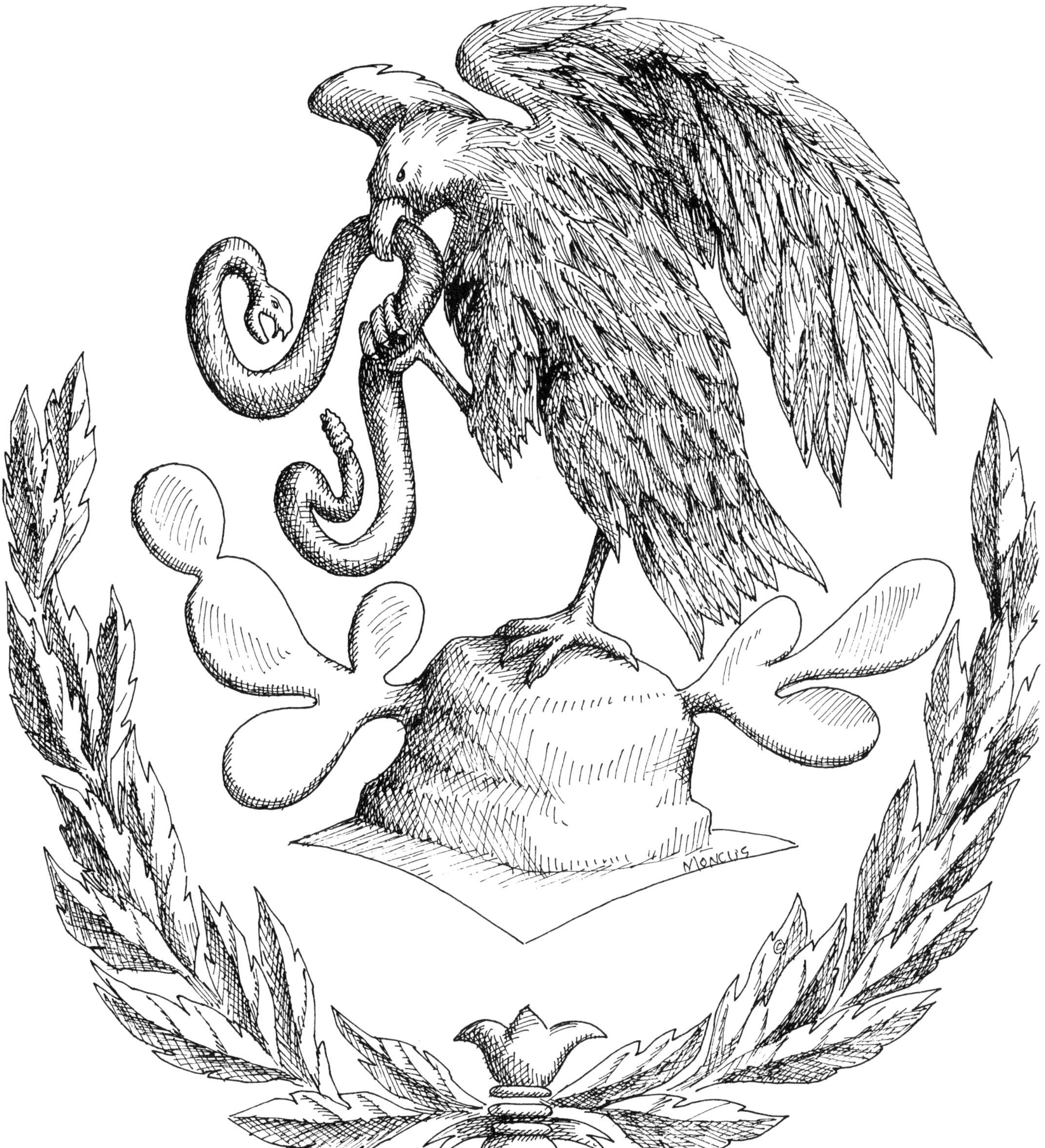
MONCLUS

IDIOMS

MODISMOS DICHOS EN MEXICO	IDIOMS COMMONLY USED IN MEXICO
A la larga	In the long run
A propósito	By the way
A tontas y a locas	Helter-skelter
Sorprender con las manos en la mesa	Caught red-handed
Agotar la paciencia	Wearing out my patience
Al fin y al cabo	When all is said and done
Al pie de la letra	Word for word
Andar de la Ceca a la Meca	Looking high and low
Andarse por las ramas	Beat about the bush
Codearse con	Intimate with
Consultar con la almohada	Sleep on it
Creerse la gran cosa	Thinks highly of himself
Cueste lo que cueste	At whatever cost
Dar en el clavo	Hit the nail on the head
Dar lata	Pain in the neck
De todos modos	At any rate
De mal en peor	Getting worse and worse
Empinar el codo	Drinks too much
En los quintos infiernos	At the end of nowhere
En pleno día	In broad daylight
Estar en ayunas	Being ignorant
Hacer falta	Need
Hacerse de la vista gorda	Shuts his/her eyes
Hay moros en la casa	The coast is not clear
La cosa está que arde	Things are getting pretty hot
Llamar el pan pan y el vino vino	Call a spade a spade
Llover a cántaros	Raining cats and dogs
Lo pasado, pasado está	Let bygones be bygones
Meter la cuchara	Butting in where it's not his business
Meterse en un lío	Get into a mess
No cabe duda	No doubt
No poder tragar a	Can't stomach
Pagar los platos rotos	Pay the piper
Perder la chaveta	Going out of his mind
Poner el dedo en la llaga	Touch a sore spot
Poner por las nubes	Spoke highly of him
Sudar la gota gorda	Go through plenty
Tener que vérselas con uno	Have to answer to him/her
Trato hecho	It's a deal
Valer la pena	Worthwhile
Ver la paja en otro ajeno	Seeing other people's faults
Vivir de gorra	Hanger-on
Volver en sí	Came to

It is a mystery where and when the name "Mother Goose" originated. Some researchers have attempted to trace the origin of Mother Goose to Bertrada Goosefoot, Mother of Charlemagne, who was the children's patroness. However, there is no proof for this assumption. We do know, though, that most of the rhymes were well known in France in the seventeenth century. In 1637 there was an Italian collection. Many of the Mother Goose rhymes originated in England and were based on folk songs, ballads, street cries and tavern songs, and some rhymes had a political background.

John Newbery published in 1760 the first edition of Mother Goose as we know it today. In 1785 or 1786 the first American edition, "Mother Goose Melody," was published by Isaiah Thomas in Worcester, Massachusetts. Thomas' book had fifty-two rhymes. After 1786, hundreds of rhymes, jingles, songs, and riddles have been published.

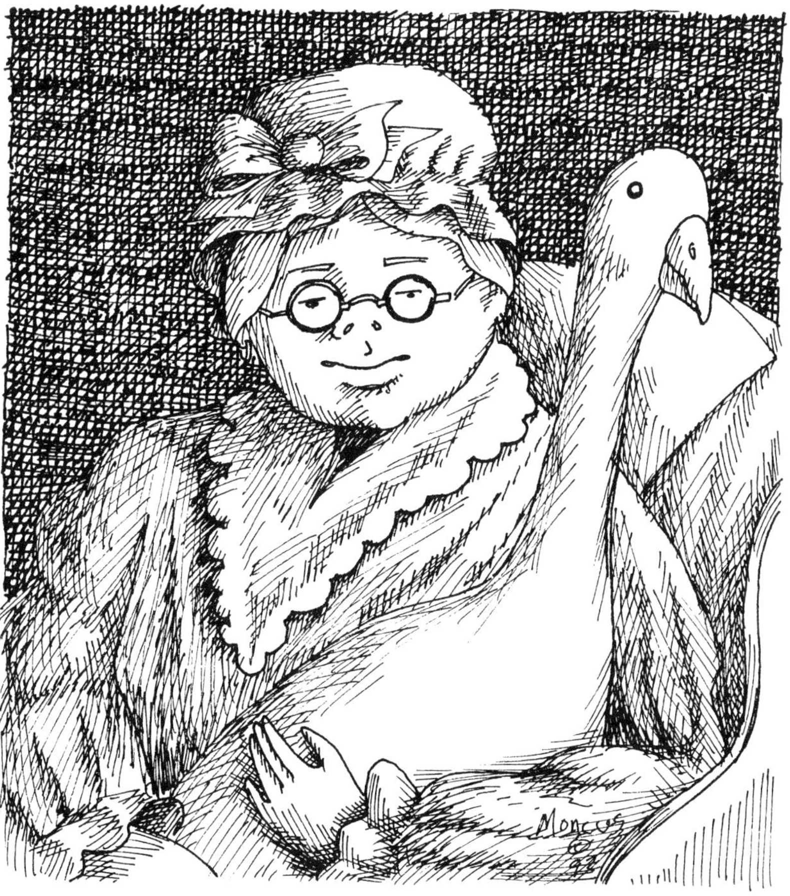

RACHEL PRESSLY DAY is a graduate of the University of Texas. She was a kindergarten bilingual teacher in Houston public schools for almost twenty years. Rachel is the daughter of missionary parents. Her father spoke Spanish fluently, having been born in Mexico of missionary parents. Her mother did not know Spanish. To help her learn the language, Spanish was spoken in the home. Rachel's early schooling was in mission schools; later she attended the American school in Tampico. Rachel and her husband, Clyde Wickliffe Day, a retired chemical engineer, live in Kerrville, Texas.

GRACE BARRINGTON HOFER, co-author of the book, is a native Kansan. She majored in drama and English at Emporia State College, Kansas, and attended summer schools at Kansas University. She is a former fifth-grade teacher and secretary for an engineering concern. For two years she was a dramatic coach of the home-talent, musical farce "Aunt Lucia," which was presented by the Universal Producing Company of Fairfield, Iowa. Grace and her husband, Clair, now live in Kerrville, Texas.

STEPHEN MONCUS, who designed the book, has done over fifty pen and ink illustrations. Steve is a commercial artist and teaches art at Tom Moore High School, Ingram.

DATE DUE			

+ SP

E MOTHE
Oyen, ninos = Listen,
children : a unique
collection of Mother Goose
rhymes, songs, jingles, and
riddles in Spanish and Engl
Central Children JUV CIRC

iccrx
Houston Public Library

7/01   8   8/01
5   9/95   13 4/10